'Guilt is like a snake…
you don't always know when it
will lash out and paralyse you.
My guilt is my twin.'

Translated from French by Adriana Hunter

brazen

THE
FAMILIA
GRANDE

A Memoir

CAMILLE KOUCHNER

Translated from French by Adriana Hunter

brazen

May 2022

1

This edition published in Great Britain in 2022 by brazen, an imprint of
Octopus Publishing Group Ltd
Carmelite House
50 Victoria Embankment
London EC4Y 0DZ
www.octopusbooks.co.uk

An Hachette UK Company
www.hachette.co.uk

Published in the United States by Other Press
267 Fifth Avenue, 6th Floor
New York, NY 10016

ISBN 978-1-91424-035-5

A CIP catalogue record for this book is available from the British Library.

Typeset in 11/18pt Plantin MT Pro by Jouve (UK), Milton Keynes

Printed and bound in the United Kingdom

10 8 6 4 2 1 3 5 7 9

This FSC® label means that materials used for the
product have been responsibly sourced

Disclaimer: Although this is a work of nonfiction, the author
has changed the names of certain individuals to protect their privacy.

To Marie-France.
For Tasio, Elsa and Elias,
and all their cousins.

And my heart is subdued, but not resigned.
Victor Hugo, 'À Villequier'
in *Les Contemplations*

Contents

Part
I

My mother died on 9 February 2017. All alone in a Toulon hospital. Her medical file says that 'she died surrounded by her loved ones' but not one of her children was there.

My mother, a tiny figure in her hospital bed, died without me. And I have to live with that.

Three weeks earlier she'd found out she had cancer. Three weeks of tests that culminated in the absurd decision to operate. A basal segmentectomy; the tumour was coming out. Rest assured. She'd written to me to say, 'Don't worry, I'm not on my own.'

My mother slipped away. They stopped her treatment, which was a misnomer, without asking my opinion or waiting for me to come and hold her hand. They stopped her suffering by tearing out her heart. She wasn't given a chance to hear her children's words, words to soothe or bolster her, words of farewell, words of love. My mother let herself die, far away from me.

I'm writing these words a few years later. I say, 'My mother died,' but as I write it, I don't feel her absence. Of course, I have a lump in my throat and tears welling, but the wrench is imaginary.

I've lost my mother a thousand times; I won't lose her this time.

★

Maybe her eyes.

'What about her eyes? Could we let them have her eyes?' I pass the question from my younger sister Luz on to my brothers. Exchange of texts. 'Clearly, everything except her eyes is useless. Her lungs, heart, liver – no one would want them. But they'd be happy to take her eyes. Are you okay with that? We'll hand over mum's eyes? And then what? Luz is asking if we agree she should be buried in Sanary. What should we say? That's what she would have wanted, right?' No time to think. Answer immediately; to make the questions go away, to make them stop. 'Yes, yes, fine, if you think that's the right thing, yes, yes, okay.'

From up in the mountains where I've distanced myself, I make the final arrangements for my mother's funeral. Luz is at the hospital in Toulon. She explains her plans over the phone: 'Jeans and that sky-blue sweater with a hood that she liked so much. What do you think? Do you think they'll put panties on her? I'd say, "No way! My mother never wore panties! Are you crazy!" We'll check!'

Luz and I both know the panties story; it makes rather unusual orphans of us. And for us, her daughters, losing our mother means worrying that all those memories will melt away. It means risking someday forgetting the image of her squatting in the long grass at Sanary with a happy sigh. Her 'Come on, kids, time to pee in the grass!' was her way of saying 'Time for bed' every evening. On the driveway to the Farm, always in the same place, 'Arses bared, three girls together, what a pleasure! Enjoy those stalks, girls! We're so lucky not to be guys!' A common language between my sister and me, an exchange of glances for the future, for a later life with our own daughters. We'll have to try to stay *sans-culottes*, panty-free!

★

I've left my children with their father, and I'm heading south towards Toulon with my brother Victor.

The high-speed train is all toddlers squealing, mobile phones, people having lunch, bustle. Forty-one years old, the pair of us facing each other, my twin and me, talking only with our eyes: do you think we can cope? I love you. I'm here. What the hell are we doing here? This is the worst day of our lives.

Victor drives us to Sanary. Hôtel La Farandole, at the end of the coast road, just after the 'paddling' beach, where I was stung by a jellyfish when I was a child. This hotel has always been there in the background. We were always a little awed by it. It'll be good, I thought to myself, we'll have somewhere to go.

I'd called the reception the day before. 'For how many nights?' Let's see . . . Going to the hospital to check that it actually is our mother that we're burying, picking up her things, sleeping. One night. Burying her and leaving. No point putting down roots.

'Just one night, please.' Words I would rather never have had to say.

A lilting Southern accent and a smile from the

other end: 'Just a short stay, then. Will you be here on business?'

A 'No' had to suffice. Otherwise, how could I put it?

★

We arrive, settle in and leave again. Mustn't dawdle. Off to Hôpital Sainte-Musse, in Toulon. There we meet up with Colin and Luz, my older brother and my little sister.

Not exactly sparky, not entirely bright-eyed, altogether disoriented but, for once, reunited. Hugs and silences. Fleeting eye contact. No need for words. A heavy sky. Each of us probably sounding out the others' reactions, none of us knowing how to deal with the pain. We smile at one another very gently.

Like a slightly decrepit but reformed rock group we drift around the hospital looking for the morgue.

We find it and a simple 'And you are?' slaps us in the face.

The words break away from my mouth, my tongue working against my hard palate. I'm barely audible. 'Madame Pisier's children. We're her children.' The duty officer's tone doesn't change, he looks dead on his feet too: 'She's not here. No, not with me. No Madame Pisier here. I don't have a Madame Pisier. I'm so sorry.' Well, that's quite something. My sister tries another tack, her married name. Found her, found our missing mother. Just needed to switch identities. 'You can come in. I tried to tidy her up, but it didn't really work . . .' Quite.

I was so scared of going into that room. So scared she'd be awake, scared she'd be disfigured, scared she'd refuse to listen to me, scared I wouldn't be able to cry, scared she'd forget I was her daughter and wouldn't let me near her.

We took it in turns, one after the other, to go check. What? I don't know. Every one of us went in, cried and then walked away. I kissed her a lot, endlessly, her soft, ice-cold skin. And then I asked her forgiveness. At length.

★

Where's the lift, and the oncology department?

Zombies looking for their mother's belongings in the hospital.

This time we don't make any mistakes. 'We've come to pick up our *married* mother's belongings.'

A young nurse pushes a cart loaded with a huge bin

8

bag: 'Here you are. It's the best I could find. I'd be grateful if you could check right now that all her things are here.'

This duty falls to the eldest. Colin opens the bag. Violent draughts of our mother's perfume.

Our brother picks out a first item and looks at us, bemused. 'A TV remote? What's this remote for?' The enthusiastic Southerner, barely into her twenties, proudly brings an end to this line of questioning: 'It's hospital policy.' Beaming smile. 'The remote goes wherever the patient goes. Where's your mum now?' For once my brothers, my sister and I speak as one, one and the same, one and the same pain: 'She's dead! How many times do we need to say it!'

Come on then . . . her phone, her clothes, her laptop, some books . . . It's late, let's get out of here, tomorrow's the big day.

We have our evening meal at a beachside restaurant. What's left of us gathered at one table: the eldest, Colin; the twins, Victor and me; and the two adoptees, Luz and Pablo. Five in all. My mother's pride: 'Five children, two births. Who can say better than that?!'

My cousin Rose is here too. She'll be there for the opening of the family vault tomorrow. Her brother,

Timothée, chose not to come. I understand. Their mother, Marie-France, who's buried there, will be open to the four winds. Did we have a choice? The Pisier sisters married first cousins. But still, how stupid to have agreed to leave them so far from their own mother and from Paris! So far from us. In their husbands' family vault. What were we thinking?

A big tableful of people at the restaurant. My sister's friends are almost all here, the ones she calls 'cuz'. Her 'cousins', the children of my mother's friends. They're gentle, kind and sad. They're here with us, but I don't hear what they're saying. Rose's father, my uncle, drops by too. He comes to give each of us a hug.

★

The next morning, jeans and chunky sweater. Extricating ourselves from La Farandole. Returning to the morgue with my sister and brothers. To get our mother.

Before that, Colin, Victor and I ask permission to go to La Plaine du Roi, our mother's last home. We have one hour. We're allowed into her bedroom but are warned, 'Everything, or almost everything, has already been divided up'.

One hour in the house, one hour in our mother's bedroom upstairs, her friends sitting at a table on the terrace, not paying any attention to us and chatting all the while.

One hour in the house, shut away in this room like burglars, vultures come to rifle through everything.

One hour in the house, during which my brothers look for memories of our mother. Not a single photo or letter remains.

I take a sweater, a T-shirt, her perfume, two or three worthless brooches.

We leave the house, once and for all.

We rush back to the morgue. Hurrying again. All five children in convoy.

In that small, disinfected room where I touch my mother's skin for the last time, life's slow progress stretches still further. My mother's brother Gilles and his girlfriend Cécile, silently here with us, to close off this parcel of time. We all hold one another by the arm. The air is scant. The room is very small for five children and two survivors. A sprig of mimosa in the coffin. The weary duty officer asks, 'I'm guessing the mimosa's going with her . . .'

Silence in the car. Toulon to Sanary. We follow the hearse. Cautiously.

The Esterel expressway. My mother so loathed it. When we were little, she used to come pick us up near Fayence, where we spent the month of July with our father. Rare occasions when she drove any distance – out of necessity. She organised the journey like a game: stage one, up to the start of the motorway; stage two, the toll when we came off; stage three, arriving at Sanary. We notched up kisses at each point. And all through the trip, like a ritual, Alain Souchon's songs were desecrated by our cheerful voices, unleashed now that we were reunited with her: 'We're getting nowhere in this canoe, you know . . . You'll never leave it all behind, and go . . .' A professional-grade choral canon! And at last, we reached the house. 'We did it! Your mother's a champion! What lucky kids!' More to the point, what a relief that she came to get us.

*

La Guicharde cemetery. Peeing in the grass with Colin, stop everything! Then one foot in front of the other. Going down the street and over the roundabout. Seeing *them*, away in the distance. Coming closer. My mother's friends. A crowd. People who mostly, at least for a while, were parents to me: Luc, Zazie, Janine, Geneviève, Jean . . . my father. They look busy, kissing and hugging one another, but stay apart from us, to one side.

For me, no one. My friends, nowhere to be seen. I haven't had time to tell them. To tell them about my pain and my terror, about the fire in my heart and the ice in my bones. About the vertiginous feelings I'll have, the nightmare of walking along this pathway in the cemetery and looking these people in the eye, people I once so loved but who have distanced themselves. How was *I* supposed to know? You bury your mother only once.

At the entrance to the cemetery, I'm suddenly lost in four square meters of space. My eyes register a mass of jumbled bodies. I bump into one and look up. I kiss Luc, who is surprised and perhaps touched. Luc met my mother at university. Philosophy and political science. Luc's known me a long time. He gives me a 'There you are, my little poppet', which for the briefest moment does me so much good. I put my arms around him, to try to comfort him too.

I cast about for what to do. Cast about for my brothers.

I'm terrified. As if I screwed up organising a concert and all these people are here waiting for me with rotten tomatoes and jeers. People step aside around me. The crowd opts to give me space in dull, hostile silence. I can't do anything about it. I'm suffocating, just like my mother.

The hearse sets off down the central driveway. It's time to get down there. I take hold of my little brother Pablo's arm and, on the other side, of my big brother's. We walk in a line, huddled close together. Victor, Luz, Colin, me, then Pablo. Forsaken. On we walk. *¡Adelante!* No one behind us. This crowd of people who've become no one, this crowd who may as well be no one. This crowd of people, a list of names.

In among this nothingness, in the distance, my mother's husband, Luz and Pablo's father, clings to Boris's arm. Mooring himself to his daughter's boyfriend. And, surrounded by some friends from the old days and some from the present, in the middle of the driveway, the two men walk like newlyweds. Death up ahead and death behind.

We advance slowly at the front of the procession. As if dancing a slow dance, brothers and sisters cleaving to each other. In between sobs, we laugh. To rally our spirits. To be absolutely sure we don't fall. 'Did anyone remember the remote? Seriously, though! What about her favourite soap! She totally needs to be able to watch TV.' 'Shit, we didn't check about the panties! And what if they put her in a bra?' 'So, who *was* the mimosa from, if it wasn't you?'

The hearse stops. The crowd behind us spreads out, opposite us and on both sides. Like bandits along a hilltop, ready to attack the stagecoach on the subtlest signal.

We stay there alone, all five of us, next to our mother's coffin, so close to our aunt, whose vault lies wide open. My cousin comes over, and she and I hug again. 'My mum used to call me "my Camillou",' I say. 'Who's going to call me "my Camillou" now?'

★

As if levitating, I attend the ceremony without participating in it. I think about my children. Trying to hear their voices inside my head: 'Why aren't we there, mum?' I cling pointlessly to my brothers as if they could stand in for them.

A Mr Loyal opens the hostilities: 'A song by Julien Clerc, as chosen by her children, followed by a few words from various friends of the deceased . . .'

'Who gives a damn, my little lamb . . . / One fine day / We'll die, my lovely . . .'

My gaze shifts towards the people standing united and distanced from us. It looks as if they want something, as if they're waiting for me to collapse, as if they'd like us to show regret, to disappear.

The speeches are empty, the people giving them hypocritical or ill-informed. My mother and political science, my mother and the way she ran *Le Livre*, my mother and her feminism, my mother and sexual liberation . . . so long-winded, and so fucking stupid. The one who sermonises to us 'in the hope that' she'll 'help us better understand' who our mother was trots out a great long, egocentric, badly written spiel. My brothers and I can't stand still; Pablo breaks away. It's all wrong, it means nothing. Blandified, toothless. Soul-destroying.

The ceremony comes to an end. At last.

Luz, Pablo and most of my mother's friends return to the house, La Plaine du Roi. Some sort of homage of their own has most likely been arranged there. Colin, Victor and I head back to Paris. Each to our own destination. I take the night train at ten. One last drink beforehand, in the harbour at Sanary, at Le Nautique, her favourite bar.

★

My mother's funeral . . . I remember flowers everywhere and seeing those people I'd loved for years. My mother's funeral . . . I remember the people in the distance, who didn't come any closer. I remember my childhood, the South, the family reconstituted.

The *familia grande*.

When I was little my mother encouraged me to call her by her first name, Évelyne. 'Évelyne…Andrée…Thérèse… Antoinette. Can you believe that? Andrée!' I watched her laugh, always on the lookout for her smiles. I hung on her eyes. I loved her so much.

My Évelyne, who was stronger than anyone else and so intelligent, was also the gentlest. Her tiny little hands dappled by the sun, the crook of her neck, where I liked to rest my forehead. She used to say the important thing was to talk, that there was an explanation for everything, that television was a window on the world, and freedom the highest value. I was allowed to do anything, so long as I was sensible. And I would be sensible if I tried to understand. To understand everything, everyone, and all the time.

We could spend hours picking the world apart. She wanted my trust and gave me hers. Our differences didn't really matter, we were one, on the same team.

★

The 1980s. Coming home after school with the nanny. Five francs a day to buy sweets. Walking along rue Madame and rue d'Assas, and finally reaching Évelyne's arms, her hugs.

I used to open the door to her study and find her chain-smoking cigarettes, with her feet, her small feet, resting on the wastepaper basket to keep her legs raised.

My mother, my Évelyne, was tiny. She cheated, telling me she was 1.58 metres tall. Not true. You could lop at least two centimetres off that. Her light-blue eyes, her blonde hair, the smell of her skin, a blend of cigarettes and sunshine, the air I breathed.

I walked around the desk and she stopped writing, asked me how my day had been, greedy for anecdotes and good grades. She wanted to know how my friends were, what the teacher did, if what I'd learned was interesting.

Five, ten treasured minutes before I left her to her writing, her research and her smokes.

She always seemed so impassioned, writing tirelessly. The history of political thought. Proudhon, Montesquieu, Rousseau, Hobbes. Marx and the Marxists. Frantz Fanon. And Léon Duguit too.

She explained everything to me, making a point of the nuances, making things seem vital. She showed me why it was so important that she, as a woman, should put her mind to this. We were accomplices, feminists, each committed according to her wave.

Then I slipped away to do my homework, my first duty. It was only after this that I was allowed back to flights of the imagination. I worked quietly and conscientiously, to make her proud – and also because, thanks to her, I enjoyed it. Each at her own desk, each with her feet on the wastepaper basket.

Her door stayed closed, but I knew she was there. On my side of the wall, I lived out her power, her urge to understand and explain.

I took my bath, deep in conversation with the nanny.

My mother's provocative insistence had gradually won over Ursula. An ill-treated Catholic freshly arrived from Poland, she was happy to surrender. 'Okay, Ursula, you pick up the children from school and bring them home to me with their sweets, but then you scram. Get to work! At your age, if you have the chance, the place to go is university lecture halls.' Instant enrolment, modern languages. Ursula would become a schoolteacher and, for the rest of my life, would be my big sister, one of my mother's many protégées.

After my bath the door opened again. One last cigarette in the study, another opportunity for us to think things over together. My friends, her mother, her sister, Che Guevara, higher education, François Mitterrand, my brothers . . . little snippets and big History. And my mother's smile.

*

For dinner we were left to our own devices. 'Make yourselves something to eat. From the freezer. Don't let's waste time on it. Domestic chores, total bores.'

On Tuesday evenings, *Dallas* with my brothers and me huddled around my mother. Sue Ellen, J R . . . and each of us chipping in with comments. We discussed America and imperialism, horses and childhood, relationships, men and money.

I had to do everything on my own, but I knew that nothing was left to chance. My mother didn't take me to the cinema or the theatre but was delighted when I went. She thought me ridiculous for wanting to learn dance and piano but cherished the idea that, without anyone else's help, I found things that enthused me. We were a pair, and we were two individuals. Neither should impose her vision of the world on the other. She loathed the patriarchy and principles that were merely learned behaviours. She taught us to spot false intentions and superficiality. She liked politeness so long as it was imbued with generosity.

My friends adored her. 'Your mother's super nice! Everyone can say what they think at your house. You're so lucky . . . there's never any orders or punishments. There's shouting and arguing but so much laughter too.' And it was true that my mother knew all of them and took an interest in them. She achieved this not by going through me but by addressing them directly. They talked to each other. 'Come on, let's go say hi to your mother in her study.' They laughed together. 'So, Aurélien, are your parents still having a great time?' 'Tell me, Charlotte, how are you getting along with your diary?' 'Did you know that a woman wasn't allowed to sign a cheque without her husband's permission till 1965?'

My mother sang songs by Julien Clerc and Alain Souchon. She spoke to me in Spanish all the time. She knew Antonio Machado's poems by heart and bombarded me with endless *Camilita, no hay camino, se hace camino al andar. Golpe a golpe, verso a verso,* adding a play on my name to those lyrics. She told me about Salvador Allende, Fidel Castro and Camilo Cienfuegos. And her holidays in Seville in her early teens, including her first romantic excitements, despite her religious upbringing. She melted with pleasure listening to a Joan Baez album: *Gracias a la vida que me ha dado tanto* . . . 'How dumb is that!'

When I was six or seven I devoured the Comtesse de Ségur's books. She poked fun at me: 'Camille and Madeleine are a couple of airheads. Sophie's the only one who's worth anything. Please go hide when you read stuff like that!'

My mother rarely handed me a book. She preferred watching me choose. Will she read? Will she dance? Will she sing? We'll see soon enough. It's her life, not mine.

She buzzed with excitement when I discovered Louis Aragon. Victor Hugo too. She was bored when I read Flaubert. Later she was delighted when I discovered the writer Paul Nizan. His *Aden, Arabie*, of course, but also *The Conspiracy*: 'at twenty there isn't a single night when you don't fall asleep with that ambiguous anger derived from the dizzying experience of missed opportunities . . . A friend of Laforgue's had just married at twenty; they talked of him as if he were dead, in the past tense.' We laughed about this permanent tension between necessary rebellion and contented observation. Everything was a source of pleasure, even every difficulty. Take Gide, for example. My mother loved the fact that at age twenty, I raged as I read *The Pastoral Symphony*, just as his *Fruits of the Earth* had fascinated her at the same age. She liked that I was a continuation of her.

In her view, education wasn't about passing things on. 'My Camillou, by what right can I claim to pass anything on at all? Hell is other people, right?' 'No, mum, no, the enemy's inside. Give me some guidance.' 'Education means allowing questions, drawing out criticism, opening up choices. And to do that you just need to give confidence. *Caminante, no hay camino.*'

My mother's happiness when, during my Ph.D, I discovered the philosopher Alain de Benoist: 'Thought means saying no.' Why did it send a thrill through me? How did she know? She laughed. 'Of course, my Camillou. But you'll see, it's tough.'

★

Évelyne was one of the first women to secure the prestigious *agrégation* teaching qualification, in political science and public law. She fought. She fought to put some depth into her life. She got caught up in it, threw herself into it and made an impression.

At sixteen I snuck into one of her lectures. My mother, a tiny figure perched on that huge chair, her eyes, her voice in the mic. 'The specificities of Guevarism' at Panthéon-Sorbonne University. I wanted to understand how such a hard-hitting woman wasn't running the world, how so much knowledge could run the risk of dying out in the echoes of an amphitheatre. I could hear her students; they admired her, and I was proud. I waited for her afterwards. 'Come on, let's get outta here!' she laughed. 'I was fantastic! Hurry up before they find out it's a sham!'

My mother, my own Évelyne, only ever aimed for

intelligence. Intelligence in a first-year student, and in her daughter aged five or eight or sixteen. She encouraged discussion, tried to convince and always assumed the best of the people with whom she had these debates. But she avoided institutions. She couldn't abide the university, with its boastful professors in long robes. Career ladder, hierarchy, co-opting – she hated manipulation. 'I don't know how the administrative staff can stand them,' she told me. 'It's all fakery and complacency.' She did admire some of them. But not many.

I remember peals of laughter mixed with anger when I was in my first year of college and told her about a minor professor who went to great trouble to wear his gown to read his textbook about legal history to a stultified amphitheatre. And also her exasperation when she found out that my professor of civil law started all of his seminars by yelling, 'The law is the law!' Setting the stage for conservative law and the deathly boredom of students subjected to the teachings of these shallow professors with all their qualifications.

I looked forward to dinners at home and seeing my mother's friends, the ones she laughed with. My mother played with words, constructed puns, was tickled by

Freudian slips and set out arguments. She loved all that. She seduced men with the power of her ideas, shouted down chauvinists, throwing them for a loop.

My mother could also stay quiet and listen. During a meal, at a symposium, during orals, she gave silence a chance. Sitting at her desk when I chatted to her, or leaning over me in bed and stroking my face. Her blue eyes focused, her head slightly tilted, her expression was gentle. She listened to me. Strength of character. Stay calm, let reason bubble to the surface. My maieutic mum.

Just once I saw her back down. My mother left my father as she could no longer tolerate his absences: 'I'm tired of heroes.' He ranted and he wept. She tried to explain to him, then gave up. My mother protected me, burying me in her gentleness and her words. She refused to hide the truth from me and looked me right in the eye. 'He's yelling but I'm stronger than he is. Of course I should love him because that's the way of the Old World, but you want me to be free, right? You'll see, I promise, I'll cope better without him. I'll be happy. You just watch.'

My Évelyne leaned her head to one side a little, narrowed her eyes: she knew everything.

My mother was born in French Indochina in 1941.

Imprisoned in a Japanese camp, Évelyne found some sustenance by eating grass at her own mother's insistence. I never understood why, because she never really explained it to me. The truth is we didn't bother to ask.

'Get away from the family,' she used to tell me. And the two of us would laugh at people's play-acting, when for the sake of propriety they aped loving relationships. She often thought, 'So-and-so's a fool' and 'Such-and-such makes me laugh'. And she would smile as she said, 'Come on, my girl, be brave, let's get out of here.' We belonged only to the groups we chose.

My lack of collective curiosity meant I knew almost nothing about my grandfather. A smattering of guesswork, a smattering of contradictions. Some anecdotes.

Georges, my mother's father, was born in 1910 and became a high-ranking civil servant who moved from one job to another. I would struggle to say what he actually did. What I do know is that he was 'in charge'. He worked high up in administration.

My mother quite simply asked me to loathe her father: 'He stayed in that job all through Pétain's Vichy period and refused to apologise for it. My father supported that disgusting fascist Maurras. Can you believe it?'

At seven or eight, I knew what 'collaboration' meant. But Charles Maurras? Probably a bastard. I could sense violence and shame, ignominy and rejection. But I didn't understand my mother's hate, the intensity of it. How old was she when she understood what her father had done? What happened? I was allowed to ask, of course. Nothing was banned: 'There's a ban on banning, my Camillou!' But I didn't exercise this right. I was galvanised by my mother's insurrection. It would have been unthinkable to betray her choices – I was so proud of our complicity. 'Run, Comrade, the Old World's behind you!'

When I was a child, my mother would point out evil to

me, and I was happy to fight it. And, holding my mother's hand, I ran.

★

My grandparents had my mother and then her sister, Marie-France, two and a half years later. After Indochina, the family moved to New Caledonia, and Gilles, a younger brother, was born in 1950. Growing up on the island, the children benefited from their father's kudos and their mother's adoration. A childhood in fine society with horses and pretty dresses, diving and swimming. The girls had already developed a furious bond.

Paula, their mother, was a stunning woman. She looked like Marilyn Monroe, a family icon. She was her spitting image. In a photo of her in a white dress next to one of the actress, the resemblance is incredible. The staging of it was more incredible, though.

Évelyne was unstoppable on the subject of her mother: 'Paula was a free woman. Just imagine! She discovered Simone de Beauvoir in the fifties, when she was shackled to a conservative husband. My father was ultra-authoritarian. My mother left him once, felt she'd made a bad divorce, remarried him and then divorced him again.

Much better that time around.' When describing my grandmother to me, my mother emphasised her ideals: 'Paula put a rocket under bourgeois conventions in the late fifties, even though they guaranteed her comfort and recognition. She fled her marriage, she couldn't take any more of her husband's bullshit and – along with it – New Caledonian society, which didn't set much store by "the second sex". She left in the name of freedom, women's freedom. She had the energy and determination not to sit around waiting to be wanted, and to dismantle an institutionalised family. I was so happy about the second divorce! I was rid of my father!'

Freedom, women, relationships, the joys of infidelity, intelligence in the modern world . . . as a child, I was cradled by these stories. When my mother and I were alone together, she made a point of telling me, 'Paula explained how I could have an orgasm on a horse or a bicycle when I'd barely reached puberty! She raised her children her own way. And the microcosm of society on that island took her for a complete nutcase. I just thought she was incredibly brave.'

There's a photo of the three children on the wall in the rue de Vaugirard, where my grandmother had her last apartment, and there's something remarkable about it: they all seem to be in disguise. My grandmother looks glorious in a sleeveless top, my mother blonde and well-behaved, while my aunt has starkly short, curly hair like a little boy's and my uncle has long blond locks and is wearing a smocked thing.

*

With a 'better divorce' under her belt, my grandmother left New Caledonia with her three children. The journey went on for ever. Weeks on the boat the *Résurgent* for the second time, complete with waves, seasickness and boredom.

Once in Nice, everything had to be reinvented.

My grandmother ended up as a single mother with no experience of work. But never mind that. She took typing lessons and would eventually become sales manager of the company she joined. In the intervening time, according to the versions she told me, my mother would hide from her classmates at lunch to eat the simple baguette that served as her entire meal. She wanted to honour her mother, not give away how tough things were.

It was here that Paula threw off the last constraints of her bourgeois life. Like my mother after her, my grandmother denounced shackles disguised as useful. She hated bras and hated panties. She never wore them. Her daughters stopped wearing dresses and high heels. Just like their mother, they'd never be 'hobbled saps' again.

They certainly turned some heads, and accumulated not just conquests but proposals. They were beautiful, intelligent and devastating, and displayed astonishing sexual arrogance. To this day, the few friends from Nice whom I still happen to meet talk about the Pisier sisters' gorgeous looks and their wild antics. 'You see,' my mother explained, 'I first made love at twelve. Making love is freedom. So what are you waiting for?'

This had a profound impression on me. At eleven, I made a point of seducing every boy at school, taking my mother and aunt as role models. I French-kissed boys and invited them to dance. With just a smile, I taught my uptight girlfriends a lesson: 'Sex is a game, not a prize!' This met with opprobrium and perhaps jealousy from children my age, but I pretended not to mind: 'Who cares? The indirect price of maturity. I've done the research: freedom's expensive, that's nothing new.'

A few years later, it was my aunt's turn to taunt me: 'What? At your age! You still haven't done the deed?' And she arranged for me to meet improbable boys tasked with seducing and enlightening me.

Keeping up with my mother's, my aunt's and my grandmother's sexual escapades . . . quite a challenge. But freedom?

★

Marie-France was sixteen when she was talent-spotted coming out of school. François Truffaut had an open casting call to find the right Colette for his film in the anthology *Love at Twenty*, and Marie-France was selected. Her career was launched, but getting away and having fun weren't enough. My grandmother urged her children not only to be playful and provocative but also to succeed. Paula insisted her daughter keep up her schoolwork despite her film career. Marie-France followed in my mother's footsteps and enrolled at law school, where she qualified with an M.Phil and a postgraduate diploma – two qualifications are better than one. Gilles, meanwhile, went to the elite École Polytechnique at an early age.

The family moved to Paris, along with their longtime friends from Nice, Mario and Zazie. There was a constant round of meals and parties, laughter and future plans in the 'little two-bedder' on the rue de la Croix-Nivert in Paris. They met new people, and my grandmother was warm and welcoming to her children's friends. And seductive, of course. An entry ticket into the closed world of the two sisters, according to old boyfriends, was best sanctioned by the mother if you wanted even to be seen by the daughters. My tentacular grandmother.

I was seventeen when Évelyne's first novel was published. I could read about the formative trip at last. It was in 1964, I think, when, with no regard for their university courses, the girls went to Cuba. My mother didn't tell me everything about this time. Perhaps she thought I was bored of it, or would rather I took an interest in Castro than in her memories.

Évelyne and Marie-France were a little over twenty. Fascinated by Guevara, intrigued by Castro and galvanised by their mother, who supported the revolution, they set out for Cuba with a few of their Nice friends: Jean-Pierre, Una and others. Individualists within a collective, they didn't subscribe to any particular party and intended to pursue the revolutionary ideal in their own way. Their paths crossed with a young French group, the Union of Communist Students, whose leader would go on to become my father.

Bernard was handsome and very seductive. He knew every poem and recited them by heart. He sang badly but enthusiastically. Songs by Aragon, Léo Ferré and Marcel Mouloudji, and old French songs that his mother had taught him.

Bernard was young and authoritarian. Strongly held convictions sometimes led to shouting matches. Authoritarianism in the name of freedom. 'Between the strong and the weak, it is freedom that oppresses, and the law that sets them free.' I would learn the implications of this.

My father had in-depth knowledge of left-wing politics, inherited from his own father, a Jew and a member of the Resistance. I can recall my father and grandfather debating heatedly over Sunday lunches, watched by my grandmother, who was a Protestant and a nurse. And those lunches went on for ever. Cucumber salad, herrings, roast chicken and potatoes, tea. An apprenticeship in the violence of words, and of voices. An education in debating.

My father's father was nonreligious and principled, brave and wounded. His parents never returned from Auschwitz, exterminated for what they were. My grandfather refused to think about it, and never mentioned his mother's name, Rachel, even though it's one of the names my father gave me.

★

The expedition around Cuba took shape, and, having visited the sugar-cane fields, Bernard had every intention of finding an opportunity to meet Castro, the Líder Máximo. But in the meantime, according to my mother's account, he planned to make her notice *him*. He wanted her for himself and insisted that she not leave his side: 'The French contingent must be united. Otherwise, what does collectivity even mean?'

When the news came that Castro wanted to meet his group, my father gloated: it was thanks to him, to his aura.

First meeting. Bernard stroked my mother's arm. Her tanned skin, blonde hair and blue eyes.

Castro's voice reverberated. He was eloquent, amusing and talkative. More than once, his eyes came to rest on my mother, and he smiled at her. And in the evening, when the group were in their dormitory, a car was sent. My mother told me, 'I had to join Castro. An order from Cuba. I was the one they'd come for.' Better still, Castro was in the car. He took her away and he too stroked her arm.

The Líder was a conqueror; the leader conquered. Between the strong and the weak, my mother was helpless.

At the time, I think my father was also taken with my aunt, preoccupied with her. Probably just a brief fling, something to amuse the sisters – it wasn't the first time they'd shared. I asked no questions. 'You don't question freedom! Far cleverer to have fun with it.'

The story that has stood the test of time, though, is the one about my mother and Castro. She didn't tell me much about it, but then there was the way she smiled . . . her revolution. In my view it's the story of a revolutionary figurehead attracted to a young woman; the story of an idealist yielding to the very machismo she was fighting; a contradiction, in all likelihood. Freedom, perhaps. But mostly just an anecdote, given that, a few years later, my father would be the one my mother chose to marry. The institution of marriage for the revolutionaries!

Freedom indeed . . .

★

I don't know why or when my parents married. My older brother Colin was born in 1970, so it must have been shortly before that.

My father was a gastroenterologist, a doctor like his father and brother, and he threw himself into humanitarian projects. Like my mother, he continued the fight in his own way. In 1968 he was in Biafra, in what is now Nigeria. In 1971 he set up Doctors Without Borders and just kept on travelling, deserting the family home.

He was never around. My birth in 1975 did nothing to change that. Nor did my brother's. Victor, my twin, my *choix du roi*.

My mother and father were stunned by the number of children soon to be in their household. 'Two babies at once, and Colin's only four . . .' Bernard, the doctor, put his faith in clairvoyance. My mother told me so many times: 'To check there really were going to be two of you he went to consult some far-flung oracle somewhere in Saigon.' Crystal ball, incantations, and who knows what else . . . 'I'm so sorry, my dear. And it will be two girls.'

The Isis clinic on the boulevard Arago. The doctor's name was Marx, which was a start. I don't think my father was there. That's what my mother told me, but he claimed he was. He would say, 'Your brother was born first.' 'No, he wasn't,' my mother said, 'you were. How would your father know? He wasn't there!' The first competition between the twins? Or the umpteenth between the parents? We'll never really know.

★

Around 1979, with the help of Jean-Paul Sartre, my father and his friends chartered a New Caledonian cargo ship, the *Île de Lumière*. Bernard set off to save Vietnamese boat people in the South China Sea.

When Évelyne told me about it, she made me smile. 'Can you imagine? Your father had a woman in every port. That was his freedom. And he wanted to make me, the Beauvoir disciple, into a housewife while he was being subsidised by Sartre! He never really got it. He made me laugh. Two babies? In other words, he was focusing on the wrong catastrophe. And I didn't just have the two of you, I also had my teaching qualification, your father and plenty of lovers.'

My father, the deserter hero. My mother, a risky choice.

*

Évelyne often used to say, 'Your father's a hero of the South China Sea. You don't have a choice. You must understand him. As a doctor, he chose to save other children. Not his own.'

My early years were built around his visits home. He was always exhausted and cursed us. He'd seen so much destitution, so much violence . . . malnutrition, assassinations, war zones. Having his children around, laughing too loudly, refusing to eat meat, or needing to be accompanied to some activity sent him into rages that frighten me to this day. How he yelled. He terrified us, lambasting us for the world's injustices.

My mother and grandmother insisted we be proud of our father and find him amusing. 'You have to understand him. With all the things he sees and all the things he does . . . maybe he can't control his anger. You can't resent him for that. It's nothing really.' Of course it had to be laughed off. That was compulsory for us. Not for her.

*

I was six when my mother left my father. Allegedly, not because of his mistresses. Allegedly, not for her lover. But due to his absences and his lack of interest. Due to his male chauvinism and his cries of 'How boring!'

She didn't tell us. She packed us off to summer camp to learn horseback riding. When we returned, she had us visit our new house. 'Well, it was a nonevent!' she would say to me later. 'Your father was never around anyway. It was a relief. Definitely no big deal.'

My father still called her in the evenings, though, and she would sigh. He yelled so loudly that I could hear his voice through the receiver. We sat in a circle around the telephone. Évelyne asked us to listen to protect her.

When Bernard came home from his travels, he would sing to me, 'She's not coming home tonight, my child, my love . . . You're so like her!' and he would ask me, 'Why are you leaving?'

Évelyne, meanwhile, warned me, 'You're not allowed to cry, I'm much happier like this. You're not allowed to cry. You're a girl. Like my mother. Like me.'

True, there was no point turning to my grandmother for support. I still remember how angry she was when we were strolling down the rue de Vaugirard one time and Victor mentioned how difficult he found the separation. 'Get yourselves home alone,' she said, 'you're old enough!' Barely six years old, and Paula abandoned us in the street. To each their own freedom. Tom Thumb twins. My mother was waiting for us back home, really annoyed for the first time. How cruel of us to have complained. 'No way I'm having stupid children or stereotypical children. Divorce is a freedom.' This divorce, her divorce, was a hard-won right for women. We were riding roughshod over the efforts of trailblazing women, my mother's courage and my grandmother's too. My grandmother, who had so valiantly wrested my mother from her fascist father. My mother and grandmother had every right to hold this against us, we needed to know that.

And so I didn't cry. I understood how they felt. And, without Bernard in it, life was bound to be full of fun.

When Évelyne left him, my father very quickly started over. New woman, new roles. New life – a much more bourgeois one. Bowing and scraping, and soon national ministries.

My father would describe to me later the Théâtre de l'Odéon one September evening – all the TV channels were in attendance, and the politicians, and the stars. Of course, he had to be there, to express his point of view and build his career. Having returned from Africa that same morning, he switched from South to North, from poverty to Saint-Germain-des-Prés. All through the eighties he put on this performance . . . but he threw up in the toilets. Completely emptying himself more than once. Too much contrast or too many amoebas caught on his trip? He alone knows.

In any event, he chose that life.

Our childhood home, the apartment that my mother had left, was rearranged. Our stepmother took up residence there. Nothing was explained, everything had to be understood. The laughter was over for us. Friends stopped coming around; we preferred not to invite them.

Whatever we did, it was never right: 'Your children don't talk at the table. Are they deaf mutes or stupid?' 'Your children make too much noise, tell them not to laugh so loudly.' Echoed by our father: 'Of course, they should learn to behave!' A glowering look: we must talk. A glowering look: we must be quiet. Yes, Daddy. And how about if I don't breathe?

We dreaded going to their place.

'Come and say hello to our guests while they're having their aperitifs and then leave and keep quiet. Wee-wee, teeth and bed.' My arm shaking as I carried someone's glass or offered peanuts to those right-wing puppets and ex-lefties who came and kowtowed to the parents. My brother's arm shaking when he knocked something over. And our whoops of laughter listening to those ridiculous bootlickers. No yelling from my father in front of his guests, but a lacerating glance, a glance to chill the blood of a seven- or fifteen-year-old. A stinging comment, always at exactly the right moment, to show up a weakness, bring it out in the open and humiliate . . . for peanuts.

*

Seven in the evening, the small hallway at my mother's apartment. A place that always promised happiness. Satchels on backs, last kisses, Sunday, our father's evening. 'You can go over on your own, you're big now.' A look from my brother. 'Oh, please, mum, don't make me go there, not to him, not without you.' And soon there were tears, and my mother trying pointlessly to persuade us: 'I know your father's faults, I know he doesn't see anything and doesn't understand anything, but he is your father. No choice. And, anyway, you know he won't be there.' 'Well then, why should we go? Why leave the smell of home and the smell of your skin, mum?' The pain didn't subside. It morphed into anger, a savage anger. Victor screamed, he screamed as if he were being torn limb from limb, as if his heart were being ripped

47

out – to think, he was usually so gentle. He screamed to bust his vocal cords. He screamed like someone nobody heard.

My brother lost his voice. Ineffectual appointments with a speech therapist: breathe in . . . and out, breathe in . . . and out. In the end my mother gave up. At last, Évelyne had a prescription, a medical excuse to put forward. An explanation that our doctor–father couldn't fail to accept. Probably to his great relief, we would visit Bernard less frequently.

*

I was ten years old when, coming home from school for lunch one day, I heard on TV that Adrien had been born. In March 1986, my father had a baby son, and I was very happy to have a little brother.

Bernard told me I could see him soon, but right now, our stepmother, a TV star, was tired. He also made a point of explaining that she needed to have her make-up done and the newspaper photos taken. 'You'll have a date on the maternity ward when I tell you. You'll come with Christophe, our photographer friend.'

The man came to collect us at last, Colin, Victor and

me. There were paparazzi outside the building, and we had to avoid them. 'Let's go around the back, through the neighbours' courtyard.' 'Knock, knock, can we come in? This is kind of embarrassing, but we need to climb over your fence. Do you mind?' Hiding, and being sure to protect exclusivity for the popular press, the favourite, *Paris Match*.

Once we got to the maternity unit, a nurse was sent to meet us. 'Stay outside for a moment, children, we'll do some photos, then we'll call you in. Come in, sir, and take your pictures.' Gone, as if we'd never existed. My brothers and I got the picture. We could see exactly what our family life would be like in the future.

I finally met my baby brother. Adrien was so cute, but I could hardly get near him, whereas my schoolfriends played with their little brothers like dolls all the time. The woman in the white coat who slept in his bedroom for the first few months told me I must never carry him: 'It's best to be careful with babies.'

My mother had a new life too. Mitterrand had just been elected. Évelyne introduced us to the man she loved, and most likely had loved for some time. Ten years younger than she was. Both of them professors of public law; soon to be in the same university. Their intellectual complicity, the infinitely tender way he looked at her, and most of all how much he madly wanted us. My heart was instantly captivated.

In the little apartment on the rue Le Verrier where the four of us now lived, he would show up with his dog, Ouzo, who we immediately adopted. John Wayne boots, turtleneck sweater, and a chain to hold his lighter around his neck. A cigarette holder or bidi, never a button-down, and ties were forbidden. His cowboy mouth and curly hair.

Born into the upper classes, married and then divorced after what he would later describe to me as 'a week of memorable fucking', my stepfather dreamed of revolution. He had just written an essay under the title 'Chile, or the Attempt. Revolution / Legality' and had been congratulated for it.

After Cuba, Chile, alongside Cuba, Chile – bearing the Left as a standard, we would soon be the *familia grande*.

*

I must have been eight or nine when we all moved into rue Joseph-Bara together. Large apartment, separate bedrooms for everyone, mine in between my brothers.

The rue J-B, where I savoured my twinhood. Victor and I were in the same classes, both forging ahead, both top students. 'Come on, let's study.' Together, pitted against our friends. Victor and I were always united, the same longings, the same plans. Victor and I and our collusion, our intertwined memories, our wild instinctual laughter.

The rue J-B, where I was dazzled by my older brother Colin. His clothes, his feet, his hands, his jokes. Dark-haired, with a perfect nose and magnificent eyebrows above light-green eyes. A pull-up bar in the corridor for his body building. Girls went crazy for him.

The rue J-B, where my older brother was the best-looking guy in the neighbourhood. The bravest too. Urged on by our parents, he soon enrolled at the renowned Louis-le-Grand lycée, while friends' children were fucking around in their ordinary high schools. Excellence as a mark of gratitude, from generation to generation. The injunction is passed on, but success not always. Colin was first on the list. The eldest of the children and grandchildren. A duty to go to bed late, to study tirelessly, and to do maths like our uncle Gilles.

The rue J-B, where I often saw Colin struggle but never give up for a moment. With my heart pounding, I would knock at his door to give him encouragement. Never disturb someone who's working. A rule that was adopted out of solidarity: 'I'm frying some breaded fish and was wondering when you'll be done.' Like a bee around a honeypot. Fussing around him, the better to admire him. Loving him as much as my mother loved him.

The rue J-B, where I remember the much-loved smell of my big brother's bedroom. I remember how I waited for his 'Yeah' before daring to open the door, and then

I always saw the same picture: Colin at his desk with a calculator and a protractor sitting on the graph paper. I'll always remember the remarkable spectacle of his pen, spinning between his fingers to help him think. 'Hi there, Cam!' A knockout teenager's smile.

The rue J-B, the cradle of our complicity. Sometimes Colin ditched the studying and the pressure. He'd invite me in to talk. Our own morsels of eternity. I talked about myself, our parents, life. He listened to me, really listened. And at night, I would go to bed with one ear cocked, lulled by the music he played on the far side of the communicating wall. 'Tonight: Billy Joel. Music is wonderful, my sister. Listen up, I love this one.'

Whenever I think of my brother he's smiling and dancing. That's the only way I know him. I can hear him telling some crazy story and dancing out our dreams. His index finger beating time to the music, face screwed up in delight.

*

On the rue J-B I would sneak into my stepfather's study after school, and the two of us would listen to Chopin and Schubert, whom my mother hated.

My brothers and I were welcome everywhere in the apartment. At the dinner table, in the living room and in the parents' bedroom, where we all watched our favourite TV shows together. My stepfather took me to friends' houses and introduced me as his daughter. He encouraged me with everything. He carried me, reassured me, gave me confidence.

Évelyne would say, 'He's a good person. Think about this: his brother died on the expressway at Sanary. He was only twenty! Just imagine, the sensitivity . . .' Being only half that age myself, I couldn't see the connection, but nodded compliantly.

He used to look at me so tenderly. 'Hurry up and learn humour and irony, my Camouche. Love life. You're so clever, like your mother. And so are your brothers, the lights of my life. You *are* my life, my new life, the one I was waiting for, the one I wanted. You're my children, and more besides.'

On the rue J-B my stepfather orchestrated my happiness by showing me how to breathe. He made me do my homework and then taught me card games. Poker, blackjack, French tarot, belote. My stepfather took me to Johnny Hallyday concerts. He made me listen to piano pieces, enrolled me in tennis lessons and read me passages from his favourite crime novels. He suggested I join in their political debates. Consensus and dissensus. Age didn't mean anything; every point of view was respected so long as it was well argued. And he so loved my mother, my aunt and my grandmother. He got the whole picture, conquered the whole family.

On the rue J-B my stepfather took my father's place.

*

When my mother met my stepfather, my aunt fell in love with his first cousin. The Pisier girls didn't do things by halves. No more revolutionaries, actors and big lawyers. But a cousin? Why not?

Thierry and my stepfather were actually more than cousins, because their parents – and how wonderful was this – were twins like Victor and me. The two men had the same Southern connections, the same childhood memories and the same points of reference.

From then on, we were basically together the whole time.

Paula, Marie-France and Évelyne followed each other around Paris, from one neighbourhood to another. Eight streets was the maximum acceptable distance; more than that and we wouldn't have known how to breathe. Gilles strayed away to the next arrondissement. The sisters spoke on the phone every day and had dinner together at least once a week. Everyone met up every weekend, at Marie-France and Thierry's place, or ours. On Sundays, they took us with them to their tennis club in Montrouge. We waited in the corridors for the 'oldies' to finish playing: 'You kids do your own thing!' Then we'd go home to one apartment or another. 'Everybody can get their own food but there's drink for everyone.' They would play Scrabble or have in-depth discussions. Cigarettes, bidis, lighter holders. All under the delighted eye of my grandmother, the queen of ideological battles and cuddles.

From then on, we started going to La Plaine du Roi, their huge family estate. All of us together, for every holiday. A family that had been chosen, reinvented around Paula, Évelyne and Marie-France. Around my stepfather, his cousin and Sanary.

Sanary, the smell, the light, the silence.

Sanary, the olive trees, the stone walls, the ochre colour of the earth. The cicadas and the sea.

Sanary, the air I breathe.

At Sanary there were two houses in the pine forests. The Big House for the adults and the Farm for the children, Évelyne and my stepfather, and Marie-France and Thierry. Two houses, one swimming pool.

At Sanary there was parched grass, lavender and almond trees. And later mimosa. Bare feet all summer long.

At Sanary there was a path edged with thyme, and my stepfather taught me to run my hand over it: 'Put your hand to your nose at the end of the path, my Camouche. You can just smell how good it is to be here.'

At Sanary my stepfather made fun of his mother, Colette, who had a little bell and would ring for the staff to clear the table. He taught me that 'allowed' and 'forbidden' were personal choices. He told me he respected my father enormously but then laughed about all his screw-ups with me.

At Sanary, as in Paris, my stepfather made my life better.

★

Every August, he invited our friends from Nice, Mario and Zazie, to Sanary. Others too, childhood friends, fellow campaigners of my mother's, former Maoists, guys from the League . . . Converted left-wingers in Sanary. My stepfather's friends also came; they were less politicised and sometimes younger. That property was like a commune.

In May each year I studied the 'Big Sanary Chart'. My stepfather drew it up and sent it to all the guests. It assigned bedrooms and apportioned weeks, amounting to far more than a list of names.

He housed us, the children, at the Farm. All higgledy-piggledy, in dormitories. Upstairs, Victor, Charlotte, Julie, Samuel and me. Isabelle and Deborah. Aurélia. Downstairs, Brigitte and Emmanuelle, Colin, David, Antoine and Alexis . . . Later we would make room for Luz and Pablo, for Timothée and Rose, for Matthias, Clara, Clémence and Inès, for Jessica, for Julia, Maria and Pierre, for Nora, for Rachel and Jonathan, and for Romain and Zazou.

For the first two weeks the Big House was for Fabienne and Henri 'chez Colette', Patrick and Dominique above the pergola, Geneviève in the 'staircase room', Chantal next door to her, Georges and Janine 'chez Micou and Jean-Louis', and Luc and Dominique, 'in the chiller'. My stepfather's friends were there too: Jean and Dorothée, Nathalie and François, and Michel and Michelle. And rooms had to be given to Paula, Gilles, Xavier and Rosanne.

Later somewhere would have to be found for Muriel and Philippe, for Michel and Josée, and for Véronique and Philippe. Plus the Chilean exiles who were supported in their battle: Carmen first, then Teo.

The ground floor was occupied year-round by

Simone, the chef, the *mamá*, queen of the kitchen, keeper of the house. There was also her daughter Hélène. And Ursula, Goïshka, Sylvie and Nadège, the nannies whom the parents so loved.

The Big Sanary Chart structured the holidays for one hell of a gang.

The *familia grande*.

*

The ritual was very soon instituted. Every summer: laughing parents and children drunk on freedom.

Good constitutionalist that he was, my stepfather established the power structure. The rule of law, etiquette, regulations – as if it were a game. 'To each their own role. I'm the prime minister, and we'll appoint ministers. Camille, you're in charge of the ministry of cigarette butts: you have to empty all the ashtrays every evening, the huge ones by the pool and all the little ones hiding in corners. Charlotte, dancing. Victor, minister of the table. That leaves ministers for French tarot, blackjack, poker, the swimming pool, shopping, tennis . . . a minister for smokes and one for wine.'

When it came to lunchtime, and breakfast too, there

was a buffet. There were just so many of us. Big cold salads. 'Help yourselves, kids. Sit yourselves down, or not. Take it easy. Watching *Man from Atlantis* on TV or sitting at the table with the oldies!' At the table, where ideals fought it out with pragmatism, conversations were always lively. But, more than anything else, oh, the laughter! The parents were done with their campaigns now, but they still believed in them. Not in revolution, obviously, but in left-wing values. Those that united them. Those they passed on to us.

We were included in all of their thinking, whether it was wine-fuelled or funny or serious. Marx, Stalin, the 'Italians'. The League, Mao, the establishment. De Gaulle, Michel Debré, universal suffrage, the power attributed to the French president. Mitterrand, Pierre Mauroy, Laurent Fabius, Michel Rocard . . . Eating, breathing, playing, studying, swimming, daydreaming, everything was political.

Coffee time was all academics, philosophers, sociologists, law professors, legal practitioners, magistrates, lawyers and soon ministers. Culture and words all day long. In matters of vocabulary, Marie-France and Évelyne came out on top. *Femmes en tête*. Unbeatable.

After the yelling and howls of laughter at lunch, everyone concentrated: the 'dictionary game' or Scrabble. This was a time to make an extra effort, to go one step further, establish allegiances between parents and children, build confidence or, conversely, back down.

In the afternoon, games of pétanque, tennis, French tarot, whatever anyone wanted, in a political jumble, with no authority or overseer. For example, sometimes, in a rush of enthusiasm, they would take us to Aqualand – and invariably leave one of the children there. The parents' favourite game. 'Shit! Samuel! We forgot Samuel!' The worst of it was, it was true. 'Hey, don't worry, we always come back for you!'

Afternoons when, like the rest of the day, an itsy-bitsy swimsuit rarely won out against nudity. Josée's by the pool with nothing on, so what? Roaring with laughter, my stepfather watched our evolving bodies: 'Oh my, things sure are growing, my Camouche! But you're not going to keep your top on, right? You're not like uptight Mumu!' (Muriel, my mother's best friend, got a lot of roasting. She didn't want to show her body, and preferring modesty to nudity, she was bullied. Évelyne made fun of her all the time: 'Mumu, prissy little missy!')

By the pool my stepfather would laugh and go for a swim. As if it was a ritual, he would first take off his lighter holder, then his swimming trunks. Once naked, he would look around for a sarong. I can still hear him telling me, 'It takes the smallest carrots to make the best stews, my girl!' He would grab a sheet and wrap it around his hips. Then, he always did the same thing: he would dive in and the sarong would slip off. He then would swim and then climb out of the pool, holding the piece of fabric, and cover himself again at last.

Meanwhile my mother did crosswords, smoked and smelled so delicious. 'Hey, Viouli!' she would say to her husband, 'Come kiss me, Viouli.' 'Viouli' was for 'I love you'. My stepfather was the person she loved more than anyone else. My stepfather, who tanned ridiculously quickly. He was so dark, so handsome. He took my mother in his arms.

*

Eventually it would be evening, but adults and children alike never stopped playing.

Dinnertime was an opportunity for the biggest discussions and biggest explosions of laughter. The parents under the pergola. They talked for hours, setting the world to rights, knowing one another by heart. Careers emerged, in all their sometimes mishandled coherence. The Left was in power. Did Mitterrand have 'children' at Sanary? Of course, and they had the best time. They plastered us with make-up, hauled us on board and made activists of us . . .

They criticised or encouraged one another, questioned and debated. Together. Occasionally they hurled insults, said something wounding, flew into rages, left the table and then returned. They might also yell at the children: 'Argue your case, for goodness' sake! Argue your case!'

Even when you were only little, it was best to know how to speak. It was best to understand that shouting was down to a lack of conviction, it was nothing to be afraid of. And to understand that you needed to know how to make your point. To learn to choose your words like weapons in combat. On every subject. Not to show your fear. To take the upper hand in conversation all the time, whatever your point of view. To know how to develop your idea every time, to establish your position and own it. At seven, fifteen or forty. Those revolutionary, intellectual dinners were a school where each child learned to come out with a riposte, but in some cases they also compounded a terror of confrontation.

Every other evening the terrace at the Big House was cleared, the speakers were taken out under the stars, and the record player turned on. Time to dance. Everyone dancing rock and roll together. In a circle, on our knees, *We will, we will rock you*. We thumped the ground and hollered like lunatics. 'Hotel California', 'Africa', *'Couleur menthe à l'eau'*. Later, Balavoine, *'Mon fils, ma bataille'*. And for Luc, 'Sympathy'. Luc, who taught me rock and roll. Luc, the friend who, according to my stepfather, was in love with my mother. Luc, the friend whom my stepfather wanted us to call 'Lucardon' to mean 'Luc has a hard-on'. Luc, one of the friends I adored, but my stepfather really loved making fun of.

People paired up; the slow dancing went on for hours. The oldies gave one another invitations, clung to each other, held one another tight. It wasn't unusual for the children, barely into adolescence, to start French-kissing too. Aged all of seven or eight, I said to my mother, 'Look, Évelyne, look, how do they do that?' She laughed and held me by the arm. 'Open your mouth. Do you want to try?' The adults thought it was very funny, but I resisted my curiosity. 'Yuck! I'll try with Samuel later, not with you!' Turns out it wasn't so bad.

My stepfather sometimes danced with his dog too. Ouzo stood on his hind paws to cries of 'Hup, here! Come on, hup, here!' And once he was in position, my stepfather would drool into his mouth, spitting long threads of saliva into his dog's jaws while Ouzo gulped it down. A little disgusting, but oh, how we laughed! All those evenings when we danced in Sanary!

Every other evening, we played games too. 'How high are the stakes? Jean needs to get his hand in again tonight.' Michel opened a poker table. 'Who'd rather play blackjack?' My brothers and I learned gambling games very early. The adults placed bets on us. The pressure was unbearable. My stepfather and I on the same team. 'We'll play together tonight. Go, go, go, poker face, my girl, don't show a thing. Would you pour me another rum, honey? And I'd like a big cigar, like on those steamy Cuban nights.'

Sometimes they would organise a game of charades, with parents and children all mixed in together. Everyone gathered on the big terrace to mime book, film and play titles. And nothing was hidden from the children! I can still remember what I had to mime when I was barely in my teens: 'Come here, Camille. You have to get your team to guess *Cat on a Hot Tin Roof* . . . Don't you know it? Cat as in "pussy", right, it's all about sex. Go for it. If they haven't got it after a minute, you'll be allowed to act out each word in the title. But until then . . .' So I ended up pretending to fuck in front of the grown-ups. Roars of laughter. Sometimes someone would get Plato's *Republic*, or *The Little Red Book* . . . which were no easier to act out!

Some evenings we headed for the beach. Midnight swims. Everyone naked, both in the water and in the car, just for a giggle.

Back from the beach, who was going to the Farm and who to the Big House? The children went home to their dormitory, a large room wallpapered throughout with posters from May '68. I would fall asleep every night, reading slogans: 'Let horned animals be frightened of red – not us.' 'Too late, CRS,' meaning the French National Police: 'the popular movement has no temple.' 'The fight goes on.' 'We're all Jews and Germans . . .' In the end I closed my eyes. Overhead, the words 'Be young and be quiet'.

Back in Sanary, the time we all voted too: for or against pregnancy after the age of forty. For! No way can everything go up in smoke! Everyone had a say. Each in his or her own way.

Marie-France and Thierry had late but premature births. First my cousin Timothée, then his sister Rose.

1986. I was eleven, and just like every year at Sanary, the two houses were full to bursting. After the dancing we gazed at the sky from the terrace. Mattresses brought out, lying outside, as instructed. 15th August that year was the night of shooting stars. Marie-France was six months pregnant. We chuckled as we thought up wishes about her next child. 'Will she be called Bérengère, which is what her father wants?' Marie-France wanted my opinion, my love. Talking to her, I got the feeling that everything about me was important. Me, who'd been the only girl any of them had had for such a long time. 'Oh, no, not Bérengère!' We made wishes, and my aunt held my hand the whole time. 'I hope you'll like her.'

Things went wrong in the night. Marie-France's waters broke. Six months is a little early to give birth. The ambulance arrived at three in the morning. My mother climbed inside; Thierry would follow by car. The nurse was concerned that Marie-France wasn't wearing any panties, and Évelyne horrified her by taking off her own and handing them to her sister. 'Well, that's lucky,' said my mother, 'seeing as I normally never wear any!' A peal of laughter from my aunt, despite the looming catastrophe. The umpteenth show of strength from the Pisier sisters.

My cousin weighed less than a kilo. She was transferred to Paris and stayed in an incubator for months. Just like her brother two years before, who'd been born early too. Their friends, the Sanaryans, were devastated, as if their own children were in danger.

★

Marie-France always nurtured our connection. She always took an interest in me: 'How are your grades? And your spirits?' When I was in ninth grade, she asked about my friends: 'Where's Théodore?' 'What's Esther up to?' 'I really like your Théodore, I'm going to call him Gontran. He looks like a Gontran.' Later she took to organising my birthday each year, and inviting me out for lunch or a coffee. We exercised together and talked for hours, wreathed in cigarette smoke and the summer heat.

She sometimes felt like getting away from the Sanary gang. 'The "family", the "king's court", is friendly, easy and fun, but it's exhausting.' And she'd take me along with a 'Come on, let's go see some people'.

A jaunt on a scooter to the harbour in Bandol. We'd go for a drink at L'Amiral, and would laugh with Omar the waiter – 'So, girls, back again?' Then we'd do the rounds of the boutiques. We mostly stopped at the one in the middle, our favourite. Escapees, the pair of us.

She would call me in Paris to say, 'Come over to my place, my Tanagra!' and I would drop by after school. A smell of Shalimar. I inhaled it. Marie-France in her bedroom, or the bathroom. We chatted about everything and anything. Tried on clothes, experimented with make-up. We talked about her man. We talked politics, women and movies. The 343 'bitches', who in 1971 signed a petition publicly admitting that they'd each had an illegal abortion; May '68; the leftist politician Daniel Cohn-Bendit. I put on her latest acquisitions: shoes, dresses, tinpot jewellery. Put on cheap clothes from the market with chic pants. A pretty top with old jeans. A Liberty print. Colours. Red, plenty of it.

Marie-France fussed about my virginity and taught me about life as a woman: tampons, rubbers, looks. 'Fewer diamonds and more tat, please. You should always mix it up.'

When Marie-France made a film about her childhood in New Caledonia, she asked if I would play her: 'Who else could do it, my Camouche? Come and do a screen test. Come and be me for the camera.' The casting director was unconvinced: 'Madame Pisier wants someone who looks like her. Here's the script, see you tomorrow with your friend Charlotte. I need two friends, two sisters, one dark, the other blonde.'

It was a straightforward scene. Harbour lighthouse, exterior day. '*Tata*, in New Caledonian. People say *tata* when they're leaving, they say *tata* to mean goodbye.'

Polite society didn't like it, but the mother in the film had taught her daughters to say *tata*. I reply to Charlotte's line: '*Tata*, see you later, I have to go.' Terrible, absolutely terrible!

'Come on,' Marie-France said, 'let's watch it.' She choked with laughter. 'You're such a pain. I can't use you!'

I kept the habit and would always say *tata* when saying goodbye to my grandmother, my aunt and my mother. When they gave me a chance to.

*

Back in Sanary we also voted in favour of adoption. From Chile, of course!

This time it was my stepfather who wanted a child, as my mother was forty-five.

There are a lot of conditions for adoption.

The social worker conducted her enquiries. 'Do you really want a little brother or sister?' she asked. Carefully schooled by my parents, I replied, 'And if my mother wasn't menopausal, what business would it be of yours?'

But first of all, their union had to be made official to secure permission for them to be parents.

A super-quick wedding was arranged, and Rocard, the

mayor of Conflans-Sainte-Honorine, was approached. My stepfather came up with an invitation, transforming the cover of the review he edited by changing the title and making the masthead a list of every family member at Sanary.

A bus was chartered, leaving rue d'Assas for Conflans in the morning. Quite a sight to be seen, all of us wearing whatever we felt like, with no one dressed to the nines! Champagne on board, French tarot, poker, cigarettes, singing. A whole family heading off to be married. The people at the *mairie* weren't used to that sort of thing.

The adoption took time.

My parents grew impatient. My stepfather didn't shy away from pulling strings, and called Jacques Chirac for help. Awkward social manoeuvring. I couldn't believe it: 'Chirac?' 'You'll understand some day. Come on, let's just see the funny side of it!' With all the efficiency of the Right, the Department of Health and Social Security gave its consent. My parents' friend Carmen set off to fetch a baby.

After so many years in exile, and despite Augusto Pinochet's hostilities, Carmen was finally granted permission to spend a few days back in Chile. Wonderful images: going back to her father's house, back to her family, with Miguel gone and the Revolutionary Left Movement stamped out. Fabienne went with her and filmed the orphanages, the search, the process of choosing a baby. 'There's a nine-month-old girl here. She was waiting for you.'

My sister, chosen by friends, soon set out from Chile, suffering from rickets and bronchial pneumonia.

The whole Sanary family was at Roissy airport. It was all noise and running commentary and laughter . . . not quite the intimacy of a birth. Who brought a camera? Did anyone think to bring champagne? Standing at the airport, chanting, 'We're all expecting a baby!'

I for one held my breath. I'd had time for an imaginary pregnancy, and, with the full weight of my twelve years, I'd imagined every possible first meeting. Three brothers, and at last a sister! A girl for me too. And this time not a white coat to be seen to stop me taking care of her. Despite my feminist tendencies, I longed to dress her up, to braid her hair and choose skirts and tights for her in every colour. I longed to show her my modern jazz dancing and tell her about my father, who was so different from hers.

And then all at once, through the big windows of the arrivals hall, while they were claiming their luggage, I caught sight of my sister. She was so pretty, so moving. I could hear clapping and cries of joy: 'Look, look! There they are! She's so adorable, he looks so proud!'

My sister was absolutely not what I'd imagined. A doll brandished triumphantly by her father. '*¡Hasta la Victoria siempre!*' he cried. A miniature beauty in her fuchsia-coloured alpaca sweater, the colour contrasting with her skin and puff of black hair. Her arms hung limply, and she struggled to hold her head up despite being eleven months old. I still remember that incredibly piercing gaze. Her burning black eyes. Her dimple at the slightest smile. And her long fingers, her exquisite hands.

My stepfather made me recite words from Giraudoux's play *Electra*: 'What's it called when the sun's coming up, as it is today, and everything's ruined, everything's pillaged, and yet the air is still breathable, and you've lost everything, and the city's burning, the innocents are killing one another, but the guilty lie dying, in some corner of the newly breaking day? – It has a beautiful name, Narsès woman. It's called dawn.'

Just like the morning light in Sanary, the light we so loved. *La luz de la mañana.*

★

My sister Luz and my parents' happiness.

How proud I was to take care of her. I was the 'big sister'. My parents were quick to delegate, and they trusted me. I watched over her right from the early weeks when she first arrived, so that they could enjoy themselves in the vast mansion they'd rented in the alpine resort of Les Contamines-Montjoie.

My mother often asked me to 'take over': 'She cries the whole time. Fucking pneumonia and fucking rickets! Take her, I'm sure she needs you. I have to go for a smoke. I'll be right back.'

Les Contamines-Montjoie, a tiny Luz, French tarot, poker and plenty of laughter. Les Contamines-Montjoie, where my stepfather took me off-piste and taught me to ski.

★

Different children, different upbringings. In Paris, the parents delegated everything to nannies, who were virtually governesses. One of them would arrive at eight in the morning and stay till the evening. Another would 'take over' on the weekend. Unthinkable for my mother to be enslaved! They could also count on Victor and me when there was no other solution. The same went for trips to the paediatrician and for outings: 'Could you take her to the park, please?' The look people gave me – so young and a nanny already! Dividing up the chores and responsibilities.

My stepfather was good at talking to me: 'I don't make any distinction at all, I'd adopt you too if I could. Stepdaughter, adopted daughter . . . you're both my daughters. Camille, my Camille, teach your sister, take her in your arms so she grows up like you, give her her bath and sing her your father's songs. Camille, my daughter, look at Luz, our daughter. *Lucesita, chiquitina.*'

*

Two years later I was in Vermont, thanks to my stepmother's scheming. A camp where I would learn English with well-raised girls. Or, more accurately, an opportunity to send me far away for the month of July, my father's month, the dreaded month. I wanted to go on holiday with a school friend, but they'd pre-empted that by enrolling me alongside the daughter of one of their friends, a complete stranger to me. Summer camp, Aloha Camp. Nothing but girls in uniform, with neckties and green shorts.

'Mum, what the hell am I doing here, mum? Oh, mum, dad is such an arsehole!' Évelyne never missed a phone call. They were timetabled, as if she were calling someone in prison. A set time, once a week. 'Be brave. Of course, this whole thing's stupid, but be brave, it's not insurmountable. Just unbearable. Laugh about it. Did you get my letter?' The mail hadn't arrived yet. 'I will in an hour, mum.'

A letter from my stepfather, a long one that I can transcribe from memory:

Camille, my Camille,

Because you're so despondent in your camp in the colonies, let me tell you about the great courage of the emancipators, the people in the early nineteenth century who fought for independence in South American territories.

There's one whose name you must know. El Libertador. Simón Bolívar.

Also, take the time to learn a Pablo Neruda poem.

Because your little brother will have his name.

If you're happy with that. We're going to go get him in Chile.

And he'll be lucky to have you as a big sister.

My stepfather, a poet himself . . .

Complete adoration for my baby brother. Little Pablo with the laughing eyes. A mini sumo wrestler, overfed on flour and water. Starved of nutrients, but so beautiful, with his aquiline nose and deep, deep eyes. Marie-France was besotted with him. My little brother, who threw his head back when he laughed. And oh, how he laughed! *Pablito querido.*

Part
II

I think I met my maternal grandfather Georges only once.

My father had summoned us: 'Your grandfather's here, come and say hello.' I must have been seven or eight. I assumed that Georges had just arrived from New Caledonia, where he must have stayed on as a reclusive pariah. The truth was he lived in Paris. And there he was with my own father, who'd just divorced my mother.

What a weapon for my father! Making an ally of this man whom my mother despised. And what revenge for my grandfather too! Rehabilitated by the man whom my mother had so loved. And a Jew to boot! The pardoned Maurras supporter.

'Do what you want, my Camillou,' my mother said, 'but I can tell you: he's not worth it.'

When my father called, my heart secretly beat harder. I ran to see them.

Beforehand, I'd spent a ridiculous amount of time getting dressed. I wanted him to think me pretty, I wanted to please him. Surely, this man who'd lived so far away was an adventurer. Better yet, an adventurer who'd missed me, his granddaughter. That was bound to be why he was back. I wanted him to tell me all about it. What my mother was like as a child. Was I like her? Did she get into a lot of trouble? And what was New Caledonia like? From the few photos kept by Marie-France and Paula, I'd imagined endless sunshine. I pictured him dressed like a prince. I imagined him gallant and generous. I could picture balls in the evening, and the sea during the day. 'Who the hell cares about that old arsehole?!' Victor snapped. 'Let's roller-skate over, then. Hurry up, then we'll be done with it sooner!'

I remember a very fine-looking man with very white hair.

'Say hello to your grandfather.' My smile, as if this were a homecoming. My eyes gazing into his. I so wanted this rediscovered grandfather to love me.

A hand proffered like a slap in the face. Evasive eyes.

'My granddaughter, at last!' Like a reproach. Or a regret. I'll never know. And nothing else.

An empty memory. Just a remembered 'I'll come back' and a sense of a scantly established bond.

Back at my mother's house, no questions, just 'On with your homework, my kittens!' Working, thinking, doing something else. Growing up without him. Compliant, I did as I was told, but I would have liked to see him again. I would have liked to tell my grandfather about my good grades, and how brave I was too. To say, 'Stay here, I need you. My parents are splitting up, it's tough. Bernard yells, Évelyne cries. And just like her, I don't have a father. He's never around. He doesn't love me. I want some silence. Take me away to your silent island.'

But my rediscovered grandfather disappeared.

Slipping away to take his own life.

Bullets to the head, with a revolver or a rifle.

Two, I think.

1986. He was seventy-five.

I was about to turn eleven.

★

When I came home from school I went to see Évelyne, in her study as usual. A knock, opening the door, expecting to find that ray of sunlight. My mother's smile. Wanting a cuddle and to tell her about my day, with my feet on the wastebasket. I found Gilles and Marie-France sitting on the floor. It all happened quickly: 'What's going on?' 'Nothing. Our father's dead.'

They were having a drink. Marie-France and Évelyne smoked a cigarette.

I could tell they were hovering between sombreness and laughter when they saw me shut down. I tried to look relaxed and not betray anything, but I couldn't really understand why they were so calm. Marie-France seemed tired, Gilles busy, and my mother detached. My mind was drowning. The man I'd met hadn't been elderly, far from it. Of course, he'd seemed a little uptight to me, but not all that old. Seriously, not old.

'What happened?' I asked, and Gilles and Marie-France let my mother handle it. 'He killed himself, baby. With a pistol. Like an arsehole.' This said everything but explained nothing. To this day, I hardly dare write it, it still knocks the breath out of me. 'But he was your father, mum!' 'Well, only just,' she said with a smile. 'And even then! Stop overthinking it, he was absolutely free to kill himself. Freedom, freedom . . . I knew he'd do it. One final aggressive act from a selfish man.'

I secretly felt lost. Surely speaking freely helps us understand one another? Telling one another everything, always talking; it's all about the truth and being close. Being closer to our true selves and to the people we love. If we talk to one another so much and refuse to shroud ourselves in play-acting, then that's so we can express our fear and guilt, our tenderness and loneliness and sometimes even our sadness, surely? Isn't this painful for all of you? Yes, it is, I can see that. And what about me, don't I have a right to be sad?

I struggled to disguise it, but my mother could tell. I could sense her amusement and her anger. As if my grief provoked her, as if my distress separated us. 'Speak up. What's wrong? You barely knew him.'

The shock of suicide. The sheer violence of the act, to a ten-year-old. Most likely because of the pain. I learned to say nothing, to keep quiet about it, keep it to myself.

★

My uncle Gilles was tasked with disposing of the body, or what was left of it; perhaps this was a self-appointed responsibility. He took a boat near Nice, I think, to scatter his father's ashes at sea. His sisters weren't there.

Marie-France conjured this episode in one of her films: two teenagers scattering ashes over the waves. The urn was heavy, the wind turned, and they swallowed the dust. They choked, and laughed. Marie-France depicted it, but truth be told, she said nothing. Marie-France, who never saw the funny side of it . . .

A return trip.

Here I am.

Off I go.

Two shots.

Two bullets.

When my grandfather killed himself, I asked my grandmother a lot of questions.

My pivotal grandmother, the pillar of Sanary, who was interested in everyone's attitude, who issued plaudits, uncovering the stories within the stories, skipped from the youngest to the oldest with a swivel of her wedge-heeled boots. Jeans and a white T-shirt with little blue stars on it. Paula would be able to explain.

Thursday, midday. Lunch was over, we were taking the lift, school started again in ten minutes. 'But are you not sad either?' I asked, trembling. Paula's misted eyes looked at me in the mirror. 'Camillou, my darling, I am a little sad, yes, because it was the only time Georges showed any courage. The rest doesn't matter. Let's not suffer more than we need to.'

My beloved grandmother.

*

In Paris, as a liberated 'Beauvoir', she'd had two great love affairs. Two Pierres, who were kind and funny. Two Pierres, with whom she didn't want to live. Two Pierres she hooked up with occasionally, like a teenager.

She'd chosen to join the Association for the Right to Die with Dignity, and had become its secretary-general. Between meetings and seminars, I think she personally went off in search of lethal solutions for people whose situations she found especially moving. She would disappear to Switzerland and return serene, sure of her choices and actions. She explained everything to me, gave me all the details. She most likely needed to talk about it, and I was fascinated by her commitment and courage.

But I also remember the man who backed out at the last minute. The one who drove her to despair and whom she loathed. She'd made the trip, and everything was ready. His request met the criteria: he was sick, there was no hope, it would obviously be a slow death. The substances had been prepared, the discussions were over. The man wanted to die before he went into a decline. She would be the one to help him, to offer him this final freedom. Then he changed his mind. Perhaps he was frightened. He didn't want to go like that. He no longer wanted to die.

★

Every Thursday Victor and I had lunch with Paula. And every Thursday she greeted us with her favourite expression: 'There you are. *Chic alors!'*

She would be wearing her leotard and leggings from the gym. Sometimes she was naked, about to take a quick bath: 'Well, what on earth does it matter, you tell me!' And she'd say, 'You twins can deal with defrosting the frozen stuff – noisette potatoes and breaded fish.' She always ate the same thing: *fromage frais* with walnuts and fresh fruit.

We sat down together at her round table and she talked about President Valéry Giscard d'Estaing and the pop singer Eddy Mitchell. She loved the one and hated the other, whose nose was too big. She praised the Americans for their intelligence, with their feet on the table and their legs in the air, a much more comfortable position than French jerks, sitting at their desks. Every minute with her was a gift. Everything was interesting and felt crucial to me.

She would put on a record and we'd dance. I remember a Valia song, *'Moi j'aime bien l'école,'* about liking school not for the lessons but for the fun. Paula would sit down and applaud us, saying, 'Don't you dance well, you twins, and isn't this song idiotic!'

I was still the only girl, surrounded by boys. My grandmother adored them and gave me support. 'Open your eyes, my Camille. Never close them. Do your schoolwork, but don't forget to turn on the charm. You need to learn to work their rules. You want the boys at your feet. Freedom! Freedom!'

She'd had a map of the world put up on one wall of her apartment instead of wallpaper. The West on one side, New Caledonia on the other.

On Sundays Paula took us to the movies. I've never heard anyone laugh the way she did during *The Gods Must Be Crazy*. For weeks and weeks she still laughed when she thought about the film's opening scene, when a Coke bottle falls out of the sky. She cried laughing. I watched her eyes crease and her face contort, and it looked as if she was in pain. My disarming grandmother.

★

She also laughed when she agreed to come to my piano recital. I must have been ten.

I had an old teacher, a very old teacher, who thought I had a gift. It didn't matter that my mother refused to get me a piano to practise at home, that she thought the lessons were ridiculous, my teacher tracked down a hall we could use in the suburbs. We played on two pianos, so we needed some space. But somebody had to chaperone me from Paris to Nogent or wherever it was.

My mother didn't want to hear anything about it: 'I'm very proud, but I'm tired of your perfect-little-girl ambitions.' My stepfather wasn't free, so my grandmother was stuck with it. 'But listen, if we're doing this, we're really going to do it. Nice manners and white gloves. And don't forget, when you shake someone's hand, you take off your glove. And you don't just say "Hello", you say, "Hello, ma'am".' Tears of laughter,

Paula fizzing with excitement. 'What should I wear to look like an old-world grandma?! Come on, let's go buy me a shitty dress!'

We turned up at Nogent, all bowing and scraping and 'Hello, ma'am'. I was fascinated, my grandmother was transformed.

I sat at the piano, marking the end of her performance and the beginning of mine. I concentrated and allowed myself to be carried away by the notes I'd rehearsed so many times, by the trust that bound me to my teacher at the other piano. I loved it. Chopin. Beethoven. Schubert. I hoped to convince her. The whole thing had to be recorded for my stepfather. My grandmother fidgeted.

'That took a long time! It was incredible, my Camillou, but what an expedition! Let's get out of here. You're a wonderful pianist. We'll send your father next time!'

Paula warned me: 'Youth is beauty. You're ten years old and it won't last. Come, let's go immortalise it.' She made an appointment with a professional photographer and wanted some pictures in the Luxembourg Gardens and some in her apartment. She bought me clothes: jeans, Pataugas trainers and a cardigan with snaps. I can remember my grandmother's laugh when, shockingly, she asked him to be so good as to photograph me half-naked in her apartment in front of New Caledonia. He had to capture my shoulders and my hair, first loose, then pinned up. The portrait needed to be blown up. And the most important part was to send it to my father.

*

Paula was all playfulness and spontaneity. I could talk to her. She taught me about women's battles and swept me along in her discussions. Looking at her, I understood independence – 'When you stop loving, you don't stick around' – and also the cost of every choice.

I will always remember the day at Sanary when she told us that, just that once, she wouldn't be joining us for the next vacation because she was planning a trip to Italy with some girlfriends. Girlfriends I didn't know.

We strolled around the pool for more than an hour, both in just our bikini bottoms, bare-breasted. My arm hooked through hers, our hands clasped behind our similar-looking backs. 'Tell me about your boyfriend Alexandre. What about Samuel and Aurélien? It makes no sense at all having just one. What about Charlotte? Tell me about your modern dance classes. You know I love it when you dance. Don't forget to persevere and to fight, but not for just anything. Don't forget to think. Always. Never stop thinking. Even when you dance, even when you laugh. Especially when you laugh. Thinking can be very funny, you know. I'm proud of your grades, and so proud of your freedom already.'

My grandmother killed herself soon after that.

1988. She was sixty-four.

I was about to turn thirteen.

Victor was helping me review a history lesson, making me recite it to him, when my stepfather came in. I could see he was beside himself. 'Have you found her?' I asked – silence. Heartbreak in his eyes. 'Yes.' I think my brother screamed. He shouted, 'Shut up!' But it was too late. 'I think she did what she always said she would do.'

I was twelve years old. I shouldn't have understood at all. But I did. I understood instantly.

I ran out, ran to my bedroom and howled. I felt better hiding myself away.

I think it's the one and only time in my life that I've howled.

★

My mother arrived, supported by my aunt and uncle. She couldn't walk. When she opened the door, her eyes met mine. And her expression begged me not to exist.

Friends showed up, people from Nice and Sanaryans. Bottles of whisky appeared, and medication, Lexomil and Xanax. And ice, lots of ice, for my mother's eyes.

She sat on the floor next to a bowl of ice, her eyes swallowed up. Mario and Zazie cried. These grown-ups, my children. Some dealt with the body and the police. Others tried to understand. Their tears forced me to say nothing. Those tears begged me to be gentle, to appreciate their tragedy. My grandmother had been a mother to all of them.

In a corridor I came across my stepfather, looking agitated.

Paula had bled a great deal. The hours spent cleaning the carpet would never be enough. I think that my stepfather explained what happened to me. No pistol this time, but drugs. Lots of them. 'Her face exploded.'

In the letter she left, she'd written, 'I'm not in pain,' and then she'd struck out these words, these final words. She didn't say goodbye, she'd said, 'Don't suffer.' She'd surrounded herself with memories and belongings.

Victor's last essay, in which he said that one day he'd open a pizzeria with our father and life would be wonderful.

★

My mother didn't talk to me. Someone else told me, 'You're going to Bernard for the night. He's on his way to pick you up.'

We had to go to our father's house. Yet again, as ever, my mother gently but firmly managed my grief. My grandmother had liberally intoxicated herself. The Sanaryans could gather together and support one another, but it was different with us, the grandchildren, Paula's youngest 'children' – we had to be kept away. We couldn't stay there. To protect us or to protect them.

My father arrived and stood before me, his face streaming. Deeply felt tears. Silent tears. An unbearable experience. This man, this courageous creature, this adventurer who never cried. His eyes came to rest on my twelve-year-old self: 'Don't exaggerate your pain.'

He stayed for a while, sent us to our bedrooms to pack our things, then took us away with him. He didn't take my older brother. Colin could stay, he wasn't in the way. His dumbstruck, bewildered eyes imposed no constraints.

Just communicated his astonishment. His gentle, poised, calm astonishment. No need to take care of him.

I looked at my stepfather, begged him to keep me there. He rocked me in his arms for a long time: 'Cheer up, my little sweetheart, it's just life, don't cry.' He was trying to give me strength. 'I'll look after your mother, my Camouche. She's too tired. But I'm here. I'll be here tomorrow, you'll see.'

We walked over to Bernard's house. We'd hardly arrived before he told us to go to bed. Our doctor–father chose drugs too: 'Off to bed now, you can sleep in your clothes. Open your mouths, here's a sleeping pill each, and it's back to school tomorrow.'

Everything was said, nothing explained.

*

The very next day after school, I went back to my mother.

The house was full to the rafters. There was nowhere to cry. The Sanaryans stayed the whole day, drank the whole day, and wept about their mother who'd taken her own life.

Victor like my shadow, Colin like my shadow. My brothers glided silently. Lost and voiceless. I remember seeking out the smallest quiet corner, the tiniest peaceful place. I remember seeking out an ear to listen, a hand to hold. But all I could find everywhere was noise. And everywhere sobbing louder than my own despair. The corridors were overrun, the bedrooms full of smoke, the kitchen overflowing. I couldn't find my mother or stepfather. Everything was a blur.

There were people everywhere at Marie-France's house too. In the evenings the family went to her place, and in the morning to ours. Josée, a recent recruit to the *familia grande*, caught me by the arm in a corridor: 'I'm angry with Paula, what she did to us is disgusting. Don't you think?'

*

The days passed, one after the other, desolately slow. I found it impossible to breathe. A child suffocated by a morass of bewildered Sanaryans.

There was so much waiting. For the police inquiry, the requested autopsy. Days and days before we could bury her.

Paula's sister had to be summoned from the Netherlands. 'Camille and Victor, you can look after her.'

This Marie-Claire we'd never met. Giving her a room, taking her for walks.

And then, at last, the funeral at Montparnasse cemetery. So many people. A militant, heartbroken crowd who'd come to pay tribute to my grandmother's freedom to kill herself.

We lined ourselves up alongside Évelyne, Marie-France and Gilles. People didn't have much to say to us, her grandchildren. Everyone came and kissed our parents, everyone knew it was the end. The end of my mother's revolution, her fight and most of all her ingenuousness. The end.

★

I was entombed in fear that day.

I've been frightened ever since. The fact that something like this could happen, that anything could happen to the people I love. I anticipate, analyse and warn. I'm frightened. Filled with incurable foreboding. And my reasoning is helpless against it.

Irrational fears. My heart pounding at the slightest noise. At the phone's unbearable ringing the whole time. Fear of cars. And planes. Finding myself unable to breathe twenty times a day. Then later, fear for my children. Fear of everything all the time.

These fears inhabited every corner of me and fed my feelings of guilt.

I was afraid of looking sad, of laughing or being in the way. Afraid of succeeding but also of not coping. Afraid of outshining Victor but also of not improving. Afraid of upcoming pleasures but also of not being able to enjoy them. I wanted to do a thousand different things – I started them and always eventually gave up.

Ever since that day, whenever things are quiet, I just wait for tragedy to strike. Somewhere, soon. Tragedy that, in no time at all, in a fraction of a second, alters reality for ever. Tragedy that asks for nothing and gives no explanations. Tragedy that you have to get used to because you can't do anything about it. The tragedy of having the breath knocked out of you, of having your life changed for ever, of laughter aborted and happiness that's dead in the water.

*

I wasn't wrong. Life, our lives stopped right there.

My mother's eyes no longer gave me anything, ever again.

The day my grandmother took her own life, I was the one that my mother wanted to kill. Her children's existence forbade her own passing. We were reminders of the life she had to live. I was her constraint, her impossibility.

The day I lost my grandmother, I lost my mother. For ever.

★

Life was never the same again.

My mother and stepfather decided to rent a house an hour's journey from Paris so that we could all be together every weekend and even sometimes during the week. My little sister Luz had just arrived. There were more and more children and friends, and friends with their children. Any intimacy was over.

When we were home, my mother drank in the evenings. My stepfather poured her glass and kept filling it. It helped her sleep, it helped her cope. We absolutely couldn't talk to her about it. Black lips. Black teeth. Cloying breath. Absent face. And often startling nastiness. Coarse words, spiteful words, devastating words. To the point of oblivion, thank goodness. Until she forgot everything, until she forgot us.

My mother would talk to me in the evening and wouldn't remember anything about it in the morning.

Évelyne walled herself in. She shut herself away in her study every day, reading and rereading Paula's letters. Endlessly crying. Getting together when I came home from school was out of the question now. Victor and I snuck straight up to our bedrooms. 'Your mother doesn't feel up to talking.'

One time I was more persistent. I went into her study to see how she was. I went over to her, and she collapsed. She still had Paula's letter in front of her. I took my mother in my arms, and I'll always remember that moment. Her forehead in the crook of my neck, her shuddering shoulders, her arms around me. I'll always remember her muted voice saying, 'My mummy, my mummy . . .' over and over.

To each her own tears and ambiguities. When I cried, my mother yelled at me. I needed to show respect, to see the choice Paula had made as a feat. Despondency meant turning your back on freedom. I wasn't allowed to do that. 'Be strong, Camille. For me, for her, don't suffer.'

1988

Bernard started work in national ministries right after Prime Minister Rocard's first government was formed, right after the suicides. Under Secretary, and soon voted 'the French people's favourite personality'.

Meanwhile I attended Henri-IV middle school. I came out of my house as if from a chrysalis. I came out of my house condemned to metamorphosis. I became a minister's daughter, living with privilege. I went through each day holding my breath. Completely disembodied.

The maths teacher, who'd had it in for me from the beginning of the year, didn't give me a moment's respite: 'You look very tired, Kouchner. Come to the front of the class! Maths will probably help you count all your money.

But don't forget about literature, it's useful for speeches. Maybe you should tell your father that . . .'

All I could think of was my grandfather with his head ripped off, my grandmother dead by her own hand in the name of freedom, ice for my mother's eyes, wine bottles that needed uncorking . . . Why was she lifeless? Why did they kill themselves? Why did they leave me? 'Yes, sir, yes, forgive my father. I'll tell him.'

Wherever I went – restaurants, holidays, beauty salons, the dentist, the doctor, the gym and even Sanary – people always asked me the same question: 'So, how's Dad?' I could have been meek – 'Very well, thank you' – or outraged – 'Oh, so you call him "Dad" too, then?' – but was always hurt and would say nothing. I didn't know how he was, I never saw him.

His new driver gave me a little message between two trips, and the bodyguard added to it: 'Be nice to your dad. I know he's very busy, but it's time to grow up!' My unspoken reply: 'I know I'm thirteen, but don't you think you could speak to me differently? And, anyway, what's it to me? I personally couldn't be happier that he's so busy. This may come as a shock, but I have a life too.'

Well, I tried.

I remember the evening Mario showed up when we were alone at Bernard's house. 'Darlings,' he said, 'I'm here to explain that there have been some threats sent to your father's government department. Nothing out of the ordinary except that, in this instance, they're very specifically addressed to you. Your father sent me. We're going to keep you under a bit of surveillance.'

Adolescence gained the upper hand: I wasn't scared, I was furious. Surveillance like no more sneaking out of Bernard's place at night? Like no more smoking in the street? Like no more French-kissing my misty-eyed boyfriends? Or surveillance like when, in the future, I'm signing a cheque to pay at the supermarket and in front of everyone the cashier shrieks, 'What kind of a name is that? Please don't try telling me you're the minister's daughter! I've read the papers, they only have a son.'

Under surveillance and abandoned. Security and insecurity.

*

1988

Colin left that winter. He was eighteen. He made room for Luz, who'd arrived in February. Paula had died in

May, and Évelyne had inherited some money. She had the funds to buy a small studio for my brother. Colin vacated his bedroom and gave it to me. He was deserting the house. To live his life. He was as happy as he could manage. Cheerful despite his first year of advanced maths and Paula's death. My big brother was leaving. When he was no longer there with me, I missed him terribly.

With Lang back as minister of culture, Évelyne also left in her own way. She was appointed director of the government's Book and Reading Service, and convinced herself she had no right to refuse.

My mother now dressed early in the morning, long before she and my stepfather used to get up. This woman who'd never worn dresses subjected herself to suits and their discomfort. She'd put on her jacket seething with anger, and embellish it with a few cheap, colourful pins for a bit of warmth. A parrot, a red-and-black ladybird. She kissed me – her perfume had changed, Aromatics Elixir had replaced Creed, which I'd loved – and said, 'Let's hope I get through the day, I'm exhausted already . . . See you this evening.' Waiting for her downstairs was her driver, who'd become her confidant and her protégé. She adored him. I handed over the baton.

Meanwhile I tried to look after my baby sister. Luz, whose life – it goes without saying – was more difficult than mine. Abandoned and adopted. Need I say more?

And I, who was a brilliant student to please my mother, gained weight. I cried rarely and said nothing. I lost my mother a little bit more every day. My father grew a little more distant every day. I thought of my grandmother every day.

Some of my teachers tried to warn Évelyne: 'It's not her academic results that are the problem, ma'am. Your daughter looks sad. That's really what bothers us.' They asked her to send me to a psychiatrist. She bawled me out. As her mother had before her, she told me I was far cleverer than those charlatan analysts. She told me that academic results were all that mattered, and I must do well.

And my mother, to whom I said nothing, drank as soon as it was evening, and she refused to acknowledge the fact: 'This is absolutely not up for discussion. It's my freedom.'

I was terrified of her death, her slow, inevitable death.

Victor asked me to come see him in his bedroom. It was after the first time. A few weeks after, I think. 'Do you remember, he took me away for a weekend?' he said. 'And there, in the bedroom, he came into my bed and said, "I'm going to show you something. You'll see, everyone does this." He started stroking me, and then, you know . . .'

I know my brother, and he was scared. More than bothered by telling me about it, he was watching for my reaction, wanting to know: 'Do you think it's wrong?' Well, no, I didn't. It was *him*, so obviously it was fine. He was just teaching us, that was all. We weren't prudes.

My brother explained: 'He says mum's too tired, we'll tell her later. Her parents killed themselves. Mustn't burden her.'

I certainly agreed with that.

Victor also said: 'Please respect this secret. I promised him so you need to promise, too. If you say anything, I'll die. I'm so ashamed. Please help me say no to him.'

And also: 'I don't know if we should be angry. He's kind to me, you know.'

My brain shut down. I didn't understand a thing. Well, yes, he, my beloved stepfather *was* kind.

I'd often seen them up to it, I knew their little games. Some of the parents and children at Sanary kissed one another on the mouth. My stepfather would 'warm up' his friends' wives. The friends came on to the nannies. Young men were offered to older women.

I remember my stepfather winking at me when I was quite young and noticing that, under the table, he was stroking a woman's leg – the wife of the communications consultant we were having dinner with. I remember the woman's smile too. I remember my mother's explanation when I relayed it to her: 'There's no harm in that, my Camillou. I know about it. Fucking's our freedom.'

I also remember after another party that a complaint was recorded. The young woman was just twenty and was asleep when a boy snuck into her bed. She fled to

Paris and told her parents. Then came the explanations. The young woman was repudiated, vilified by my mother and stepfather, who were appalled by such vulgarity. And I was told how to interpret this episode: the girl had blown it out of all proportion.

But was it allowed with my brother too?

*

Over one year. Several. Two or three? I don't know.

In Paris. At Sanary.

My stepfather would go into my brother's bedroom. I could hear his footsteps along the landing and knew he was going to him. And in the silence, I imagined. That he might ask my brother to caress him, or suck him.

I waited. I waited for him to come back out of the bedroom, full of unfamiliar and instantly despised smells. He then came into mine. My new bedroom, which was now between Victor's and our parents'. The tollgate room. The forced-witness room. For those long years.

My stepfather came into my room probably to be sure I said nothing, and he would sit on my bed. 'Did you put panties on?' he would ask. 'You know I don't want you wearing panties at night. It's dirty. That part of you needs to breathe.' He would say, 'You know, every day's a victory for your mother. Every day is a day she's won. Let me do things my way. We'll manage.'

He came into my bedroom, and thanks to his tenderness and the close bond between us, thanks to the trust I had in him, he very gently, using no violence, instilled silence in me.

★

Guilt is like a snake. You expect it to uncoil in response to certain stimuli, but you don't always know when it will lash out and paralyse you. It wends its way, marks out its routes. Guilt insinuated itself inside me like a poison, and soon it had invaded every part of my mind and heart. Guilt moves from one object to another. It adopts several faces and can make you regret everything and anything. My guilt has several ages, and celebrates all its birthdays at the same time as me. My guilt is my twin. It was a new twinhood.

And first of all, guilt drowns memory. It erases dates, leaving its prey in the dark. Neither Victor nor I can pinpoint for sure how old we were at the time. Fourteen, I think.

*

It was at that age that my guilt was begat by lies. It was light-footed. I lied to my mother and didn't like doing it, but I wanted to move forward, to have fun. Of course, there had been the two suicides and the terrible distress this had caused my mother and her siblings; of course, the wind had already been knocked out of my sails, but my insides weren't tied in knots yet.

In year nine at school there was Esther, Paul, Vincent and Théodore. We were the Famous Five. Or that's what people called us: 'Those guys are always together.' We wanted to be together. All through the day we wanted to be together. They were at Montaigne when I was at Henri-IV, but we met up for every lunch break and as soon as school was out. We met up to do our homework, for a coffee, for Dave Brubeck or Astrud Gilberto, to talk, to do our hair, to get dressed up, to read, sing and breathe. We met up to dance – a lot. There wasn't a single night I slept alone. No matter whose house we were at, we slept together. All the time. We loved ourselves as a group. We loved one another completely. I loved them, but not a word, I told them nothing.

In year nine I abandoned my brother. That I do remember. Having been so afraid for my mother, I escaped the house and abandoned my twin. For the first time. Victor wasn't involved in my friendships. He wasn't there. Not part of my life. In year nine I still had my nerve and I put my trust in freedom. I left. The freedom of a twin set loose, a loose-cannon twin. There were four people who allowed me to break away from twinhood, to leave Victor.

It was only later that I would hate myself for leaving him. Only a few years later that the snake would start to dance.

As well as intellectuals, ministers started visiting Sanary. All playing pétanque, being bawled out by my stepfather, who was supercharged and having fun. My mother hung back. My stepfather ruled the roost even more than before.

He would tell anyone prepared to listen that he was now an adviser to the president of the Constitutional Council, the highest jurisdiction.

He made sure he was king in court and in the city. And he was the *roi*, the king, in La Plaine du Roi.

With each passing summer his friends changed. It has to be said, he had a knack for driving away the disloyal. Unless it was the other way around, and they chose to stop taking part, replaced by other people. Fabienne and Henri came less and less. And like Luc, Patrick would soon stop coming. Gilles had long since drifted away. Rosanne was buying her own house nearby. Later, Marie-France and Thierry would leave, but they wouldn't go far either, buying their own place fifteen minutes from Sanary.

In 1990, the revolutionary socialists made way for the champagne socialists.

Power pays. State schools were now out of the question for the children. Luz, Pablo and all the 'cousins' were enrolled at the private École alsacienne, even though I'd been taught to despise the place. The children also worked their parents' network.

At Sanary, the recent French prime ministers Rocard, Cresson, Bérégovoy and later Jospin would find more fans than Castro and Allende. Fans of power, often born social climbers.

My stepfather intended to anchor all these people in his obsessive identity. The *familia grande* had a protected designation of origin, like fine wine.

And to achieve this he used my mother and her past allegiances. Even when she died, he would display photos of her and Fidel. Even my father would be framed, in among the lovers. Later, although my stepfather didn't understand a word of Spanish, he would arrange for his Chilean friend Teo to sing. And this propaganda worked . . . for a long time, and increasingly effectively.

A former fling of his – 2010 vintage, I'd say, from the batch of political editorial writers or perhaps ill-informed journalists – would trot out the words 'We are the *familia grande*' at my mother's funeral without understanding their significance. The left wing, living it up on the Left Bank. The *familia grande* in Saint-Germain-des-Prés. These people didn't know who we were. I never properly met most of them.

In 1990 we could no longer all sit down for meals at Sanary. Too many people. Dinner for the children, the youngsters, then dinner for the grown-ups. I was now with the oldies.

Only just fifteen and smoking with my parents. Nothing was forbidden at Sanary. My mother bought me packs of cigarettes but thought my father should pay for them. Truth be told, we smoked pretty much anything.

Only just fifteen, when my stepfather appointed himself photographer. Arses, breasts, skin, fondling – it was all captured, and blow-ups of the images were exhibited on the walls of the Farm. In the kitchen of that house where the children slept hung a photo of his old mother as good as naked in the jacuzzi, her breasts floating on the surface of the water. A square-shaped close-up of mine, and one of my sister's arse as she ran down the path. 'I don't like your mouth, my Camouche,' he told me. 'Your lips are too thin. It's unnerving.' I hated my body.

★

What with all this rowdy tumult, my mother would shut herself away in her room or by the pool in her skimpy bikini bottoms, with her Scrabble and crosswords. Here she didn't need to talk, she was safe. She let her husband do as he pleased. And was grateful to him for it.

My stepfather would later have a third house built on the estate: the Maison Rouge, the Red House. A ready-made name. The myth could live on.

There he installed Hélène, daughter of Simone, who ran the kitchen at the Big House. 'You can live here all year-round,' he told her, 'but you'll need to do your bit and help the *familia grande*.' Ever since Hélène moved into the Big House with her mother, my stepfather had said, 'Hélène's like a sister to me.' A sister he put to work all day long.

That was when the evenings changed. The children were asked to make themselves scarce. Here's to a night out! 'It's eleven o'clock, pussycats, you're allowed to go clubbing.' Once, twice, then every evening. 'You take them, Hélène, and get them home . . . Sure, they're young, but we're their parents and we've decided it's okay. Life isn't meant to be boring. If you think the young are decadent, you should set your sights on a bit of freedom!'

Destination clubland! We went by car. Between Sanary and Hyères or Saint-Tropez we had more than forty-five minutes to put on our make-up, turn ourselves into adults and make ourselves look as if we were allowed in.

We danced and flirted and drank.

At four or five in the morning we headed back. I don't remember who was driving or who, blind drunk, puked on the car door on the motorway. Our parents had no idea where we were. We made a detour to go sing an Amina song under Hélène's boyfriend Daniel's windows. We danced in the dark, singing.

And the next day my mum came to wake us. She

would open the shutters with a cigarette hanging out of her mouth, killing us already with its asphyxiating smoke: 'Well, who gives a damn, my little lamb!' 'On your feet, you twins! It's one o'clock. Make sure you're ready for lunch. So, did you have a good time?'

★

First and foremost, wanting peace. Then to protect my mother. No more dramas, I beg of you. Secrecy took root by default. Not a word to my parents, not a word to the family, not a word to my teachers, not a word to my friends. Not even to the rest of the Famous Five, Esther, Théodore, Vincent and Paul. Nor any others after that.

Thinking that freedom meant living 'like grown-ups'.

Nothing should be surprising for an intelligent child. Colin was in his early teens when my mother sent one of her female friends, a devoted Sanaryan, to pop his cherry. Twenty years older than him, whoops! My brother was flattered but mostly terrified.

Meanwhile, encouraged by my parents, I'd been massaging the older children since I was little. For hours on end, whole afternoons, by the pool and in the dormitory, I'd stroke and scratch and release tension.

One of those children would later tell me, 'I was twelve when your stepfather came and French-kissed me at Sanary behind my parents' backs. I didn't say a word.'

Believing we were lucky to have people like *that* around us.

Year ten. My concentration and energy were burned out. Contrary to what the teachers said, I did knuckle down. Contrary to what those who spoke to me said, I did listen to them. But I'd stopped hearing anything. I'd stopped understanding anything. I didn't even understand why. The blackboard was torture, especially in science. Any logic was beyond me.

At the end of year ten, I disappeared. I dissolved so I could be all the quieter. I wasn't up to my mother's expectations. I wanted to focus on literature, and she wouldn't agree to it. She told my father, who was exasperated. The teachers at Henri-IV groused, 'She could do better if she just worked a little. We won't have her doing sciences. She can do her science stream at

Fénelon if you're planning on forcing her. But her brother can stay here.'

Year ten. A blank year. A year of cotton wool and overexposed light. Year eleven wasn't much better. Nothing to be done about it. I let life have its own way.

I let my mother have her own way: 'Your brother Victor is leaving. He wants to go. He's such a fucking pain. Viouli's made all the arrangements, he's found him a room in the apartment block over the road. You two are only seventeen, but I want him to go, I want him to stop criticising everything.'

With no Victor at the house any more. I was torn. Colin was long gone. I'd lost my brothers. Left alone to face my mother and stepfather, along with Luz and Pablo. And my secret.

*

I assume the incest stopped when Victor left, but I can't be sure. My brother broke away, and I no longer really knew what went on.

For me, the years after that were a time of permanent vigilance. A time of duplicity and dissociation. A time of violent contradictions. Anger didn't surface straightaway.

There was a persistent inability to understand, followed by a silence, that went on for even longer.

The years after that were a time of guilty adoration.

For all those years, I did more than keep quiet, I protected my stepfather. Particularly when my brother decided to stop him, when Victor told me he was trying to get away from him: 'I don't give a damn about that arsehole, just act like nothing happened. Do it for Évelyne. He'll kill himself too and she won't be able to handle it.'

For all those years, and long afterwards, I protected my stepfather.

Not because my brother had asked me to but because I loved him like a father and – in our atomised family and confronted with my mother's downward spiral – he was all that I had left.

Because he organised our holidays, took us to the cinema and would soon be teaching me about law.

Because all through my childhood, all through my teens and after the suicides, my stepfather was there for me. Because he knew what Paula whispered to me, what my mother taught me and what Marie-France meant to me. Because he tried his best to pick me back up again.

Because he was the only person to give me that. Because he knew me by heart, with his heart.

★

Those years went by calmly, in silence. And yet they were years of unvoiced screams.

Alongside my mother, I erased myself. Keeping quiet was my way of sounding the alarm for her.

Once, during dinner when we were on a 'post-suicide saltwater spa break', I told her, 'I'm here but I'm not here'. Even though it was the first time we'd had some time alone together. A spa ritual after the revolver and the drugs. A week of just the two of us to help my mother stop drinking. A week during which she suffered and worked relentlessly. A week of supporting her. A week with old people, all tidy hair and coughing, boring old people. A week far away from my brothers. A week when I was co-opted to protect my mother.

Of course, she wanted to hide it. She was ashamed of the expense and told me, 'I'll pay for this for you, but promise me you'll lose three kilos.' We ate nothing and spent all day in the water. Wet swimsuits, prune-like fingers and guaranteed fungal infections. Wearing robes, bored shitless. We tried not to be at each other's throats.

I drifted. I floated. Skimming over the top of reality. But when, one mealtime, she said, 'We're both bored, you could talk to me' and insisted I come back down from this absent state, I was speechless. My brain sent me the data: we were there, she was there, I was there. I had to talk.

What could I say to my mother whom I loved so dearly? 'I'm here, mum, but I'm not here'? I couldn't think of anything else. I wanted to talk to her but had nothing to say to her. Nothing came to me. Évelyne got angry, saying, 'How could you? Do you know how brutal you're being? I invite you to this place and you can't bring yourself to be here with me.' She cried. Without alcohol, she cried. Without her mother, she cried. And I was there, but I wasn't there.

1995

I was twenty.

Colin went off to live in Texas, Victor in Madrid. I stayed in Paris. Paralysed. Anaesthetised.

Victor left by car. Standing on the pavement, I could feel my stomach turn inside out. Our first 'I'm leaving' separation. Our first 'I'm relying on you, Camille, to make sure nothing falls apart, I'll be back' separation.

Colin was too far away for me to call him. We wrote each other thoughtful, chatty letters that helped me keep it to myself and say nothing.

Leaving was a lucky break for them. A relief, even. I didn't resent them. But I was alone and realised, for the first time, that I always would be.

★

The shadow in my mother's eyes, a shadow tinged with sadness and hostility, didn't fade. I could see her pain. I had trouble breathing. She resented everyone, but most of all those closest to her. She didn't say so, but I could feel it. She resented us for forcing her to live. Exasperated by those of us who managed to survive.

My mother even lashed out at her sister.

Marie-France was doing better. She'd decided to take a role in Paul Claudel's play *Le Père humilié*. Later she did some Sacha Guitry. My mother thought she could force her to give it up, so she insulted her, humiliated her: 'Claudel's a despicable old reactionary! How could you do that to mum? Didn't you learn anything? Don't you have any critical faculties? Art doesn't justify everything. Don't give up the ideological fight. Be brave. Which side would you have been on in 1940?' And 'That misogynist Guitry!' Marie-France was horribly hurt.

My mother didn't go to watch her perform, and issued instructions that I wasn't to go either, without any explanation. The press raved, the plays were successes.

From then on, I went to see Marie-France in every role she played, regardless of what my mother said.

*

I left the family apartment in my first year of law school.

I stopped going to classes. What was the point? I worked at home, alone. And studied the day before exams.

I turned my personal life into something violent. At least in that one area I granted myself the right to decide. It was my own battlefield. My private life.

My boyfriends were never in a good place, and that was what interested me about them. By and large, I was ill-equipped to sustain friendships; I would be all over someone, then I'd disappear. My friend Charlotte resented me for it. Others followed suit. I know they did.

The boys I chose were shooting stars. That was my only condition. Not one of them was allowed to stick around. Not one was allowed to dig deeper. I saw their indifference as the only mark of respect.

I dropped into my mother and stepfather's apartment like a ghost, to reassure them and give them a hug.

My mother was teaching again and worked all day.

I tried to look out for Luz and Pablo. Victor and I had promised each other we'd be vigilant.

The Department of Health and Social Security had advised that, with adopted children, it was best for them to have psychiatric support from a very young age. A good idea at last. Victor called Pablo's therapist to check that nothing had happened to our little brother, and told him about the assaults. The shrink cut the conversation short – 'You have no right to call me. You're not my patient' – and didn't say a thing. Luckily, that particular therapist stopped practising soon afterwards.

So, Luz and Pablo were seeing specialists, and I told my mother that I would take them to their appointments. I was watching over them, Victor explained. Later, my mother would write a book to complain about my brother and adoption and her terrible difficulties.

I had no moorings. I was distanced from myself and from them, as if on drugs. I had nothing to cling to. I was constantly lost in thought, but my head was empty. With my brothers gone, I let go of reality. And I was still chasing the same dream: being forgiven.

★

I think it was at this point that the snake's heads started multiplying. It's hard to say exactly when and how.

Until I was twenty, the hydra had simply been a snake, a reptile that fostered my bewilderment. I was nowhere. Absent even when I was present. I'd lost interest in everything and couldn't make decisions. I just wanted not to be there. Not to exist, in fact. Enrolling at law school was easy: I was trying to be like my parents so that I couldn't criticise them. It was as simple as that. Long, slow years spent in chains and boredom.

Then the hydra invited itself in, became more persistent and displayed new characteristics. Sadness joined the initial stupefaction, then came the anger. Sadness for my mother and anger with myself. A vast sense of guilt for being alive.

*

Alone in Paris, I watched my mother. Alone in Paris, I tried to reconnect with her. I was the only person she had left to undress with her glorious blue eyes. We could keep up our old habits. 'C'mon, let's go to the café down the road.' The best times, getting together over cigarettes and coffee, over scratch cards. We just sat there scratching. 'So, still no cute guy to get your teeth into, my Camillou?'

We talked about university and heroes. She gave me news of Marie-France, Gilles, Rose and Timothée. She couldn't wait to go and take up residence at Sanary, as she did every summer. She talked to me and laughed, she was happy again, almost light-hearted, even though her parents' suicides had changed her for ever. I recognised the filter in her eyes, and now accepted it.

'You're my bare essential, my Camillou.'

Her newfound happiness released in me a guilt that couldn't be shifted, an untreatable festering wound, an inconsolable pain. My mother's expression and her joy tore me apart. I felt dirty, dirty for life. Her longing for a close connection tortured me, and my shame obstructed it. The hydra permanently precluded any indulgence or spontaneity.

My guilt was born of secrecy and lies. I can't talk to you. I'll lie to you for the rest of my life. The hydra's heads danced. I'm guilty of lying to you the whole time. That thought had a stranglehold on my brain, meaning I no longer had any hopes. And I'm going to let you down, you, the person who taught me the truth and the courage to criticise. Does thinking mean saying no? You should set your sights on a bit of resignation.

*

Then the hydra displayed another characteristic. The snake struck during our silences and our eye contact: I was guilty of participation.

The burning in the pit of my stomach, a constant surreptitious torture, carved up my brain. And several times a day the guilt would boil over and sweep aside my paralysis: by not pointing out what was going on, I had participated in the incest. Worse than that, I'd stood by it. 'Misnaming things adds to the misfortunes of the world.' I know, mum.

My guilt was the guilt of consent. I was guilty of not having stopped my stepfather, of not having understood that incest was forbidden.

*

The hydra spread further. The violence of shame was added to the mix. I would look at my mother and feel ashamed of what had happened. Along with Victor, I accepted this fact: he wasn't the only one who'd allowed himself to be manipulated. He wasn't the only one who'd betrayed my mother. Because at fourteen I'd chosen to say nothing. Because at fourteen, and for a long time, I'd chosen to cling to my stepfather's love rather than distance myself from it.

The guilt that my brother carries in him is something I carry too. I knew, and I didn't want to stop it. I knew about it, mum. The way my stepfather looked at me, his affection and the father that I'd made of him made me an accomplice. I accepted it, perhaps even wanted it. I was cornered.

And this thought itself immediately produced remorse for stealing something from my brother: the violence that he alone had suffered.

★

The monster was perverse. It disseminated lies: 'This isn't your battle. You were just the custodian of a childhood secret, you have no right to complain. Nothing happened to *you*. Your claims have no legitimacy.'

It was impossible to defeat the hydra so long as I didn't believe I was a victim.

And in my ear, my mother singing Julien Clerc: 'Don't say a word, promise me please, about my childhood memories . . .'

Part
III

I was twenty-five and I'd loved him a good while already.

I was twenty-five when Thiago finally kissed me.

I was twenty-five and I wanted to forget everything.

I was twenty-five and, perhaps because we were being sentimental or romantic, Thiago allowed me to choose life.

At a restaurant table in Pamplona, Marie-France indicated I should meet her in the ladies' room. 'Oh, my girl, have you lost your mind?! You're totally crazy about this guy. I see you. Get out your lipstick for me!' When I did as she asked, she squawked, 'Not *here*, you klutz! You put lipstick on in front of men. It's a performance meant for them!' Marie-France the actress, Thiago the screenwriter. Marie-France by my side.

At the time that Thiago kissed me, he was producing American films on French soil. My father called him an entertainer. My mother melted at the sight of him but warned me against the deceptions and snobbery around him. And she was worried too: 'You'll be eaten alive by his family, my girl!'

Thiago's father had wanted him to go into industry or politics; mine wanted me to be a lawyer. With Thiago, I could dream of music and words. Jonathan Richman, David Bowie and Bob Dylan. In my life at last. My father might conclude that I had no ambition, and I was well aware of his paradigm.

Watching old American movies. 'Didn't your parents show you *anything*? Don't worry, we'll play catch-up.' 'And I'll keep you entertained, Thiago, I'll describe the mother I love, the one who's been free for a long time, and who opens bottles by cracking them against a stone or asking me to do it.'

Thiago was funny, cultured, talented, a musician, sexy, a dancer, wonderful. Thiago was a dream, a dream that distanced me from reality.

We laughed together. Social status and power – fine!

People all do exactly as they please. But, for the two of us, thanks, but we'll stay away from our parents' plans.

Like Marie-France, I was drawn only to elegance. The elegance of humour and generosity, of literature and music listened to again and again, of images and the narratives that go with them, of the world of ideas that allows us to break away.

The elegance Thiago displayed with his creativity and his reserve.

But this predilection was shrouded in silence and secrecy.

The first decade of the new millennium – I spent it making things up. I spent it lying.

With Thiago by my side, I did what I could. Said nothing. Listened, understood, questioned. I said nothing about my life, nothing about myself. For my brother's sake, and my own, I tried to be cheerful.

★

I was twenty-five and my law thesis was coming along.

I'd met Pauline and Maya, Ph.D students under the same advisor. My free and studious alter egos, new friends with whom I spent my days. We met up to work and laughed a lot. Our sessions spent researching and writing produced the LKR, the initials of our family names. We drank gin

142

and tonics while reading Jürgen Habermas and Gunther Teubner. We sometimes drafted our theses on toilet paper wrapped around us. We each had our own subject, our own individual path. Economic reasoning in law, procedure, opposability – I couldn't give a damn about any of it!

'Obviously, you deserve it, but watch out,' Maya warned me. 'People at college resent you already. A research grant, and tongues are wagging about you. They're saying, "The minister's daughter gets a grant – that must be a fix. Have you seen how haughty she is!"'

Employment law that predicates questionable, unequal choices. David against Goliath. Employment law, a branch of the law that mistrusts the consent of one of the parties and tries to protect the weak against the strong, to rebalance their choices. A perfect find for me. I was impassioned, and time accelerated.

But I was still a prisoner.

My relationship rattled me. Intimacy necessitated questions, which came with increasing frequency. I had 'someone', someone who was in love with me, perhaps someone I could confide in . . .

★

Victor summoned me regularly, wanting me to know about his therapist and his nightmares. He described his rare conversations with our stepfather, who refused to apologise and told him he was feeling so terrible he might take his own life. Victor relayed our stepfather's imploring him, insisting he keep everything from our mother and the rest of the *familia grande*.

And Victor reminded me regularly, 'If you give up on me, I won't cope. If this gets out, Bernard would be angry with us. If this gets out, I wouldn't be able to go anywhere without being stared at. If this gets out, everyone will know. Come, I need to talk to you, but you, you have to say nothing, please.'

My brother who needed me, but I didn't know what to do for him.

My mother would call me in the evenings, drunk. Her mother was dead . . . she hurled insults at me. And then forgot.

*

Victor was twenty-five and had a truly brilliant career. His work was his escape mechanism. He worked relentlessly, morning and evening. I was happy for him.

But I could see that my brother wasn't really there. In the slow process of rebuilding themselves, victims continue to believe they're guilty for a long time. A classic process that I instinctively grasped and understood. In all probability I was going through it too. I gave him time. Time to understand it wasn't down to him at all. Later, a charlatan therapist would persuade me to keep quiet about it: 'Your brother's word has already been violated once. You can't do it a second time by speaking for him. He's telling you no. You must respect that no. It's not your story.'

I stayed voiceless, confined. If this silence was to last, it was out of necessity.

Victor had a son. My first nephew, and Évelyne's first grandchild. 'Come on,' Victor said to me, 'let's go to Sanary. For Évelyne's sake. She won't understand if we don't. We can stay at the Farm, it'll be fine. Our parents'll be at the Red House, but we won't be. We won't eat together in the evenings or at lunch. We'll just see each other sometimes, that's all. Please. For Évelyne.' I headed south towards the cicadas with him. Not too worried, glad of an opportunity to show the place off to Thiago.

The first decade of the new millennium. Victor and I hadn't taken the same path.

Victor had lightened his load by marking out his trajectory. For a long time, I thought he was running away, but the truth was it was all very carefully thought out. Not as I would have wanted it, but in his own way, with a great deal of courage and perseverance. Victor threw himself into his career and told me, 'I hate that arsehole and I don't want to hear his name again.' He had three children and told me, 'This is my life. I don't care about the rest because there's nothing we can do about it.'

Meanwhile I detached myself from the *familia grande* with Thiago. But unlike my brother, I had trouble believing in myself without them. I also struggled to cope with all those dinners and birthdays and the fake closeness that would continue to fuel our day-to-day lives for years to come. I found faking painful.

The first decade of the new millennium. My memory had holes in it. When things were too tough, my memory punched a hole in itself. And my brother did the same. A lot.

But if I'm reminded of particular incidents, I still sometimes remember them. I remember, for example, our thirtieth birthday dinner, when our stepfather pretended to be a big fan of my father's and he – Bernard – reciprocated without even realising it.

I've always known how to keep quiet about it, but what became difficult to accept was continuing to reassure them all. Particularly as, with Thiago and thanks to him, I had better things to do and better things to invent.

★

Thiago had a son, my stepson, who taught me to breathe again. My real blended family. Thiago had a son who'd always tried to understand, to get to the bottom of things, ever since he was tiny. Thiago had a son I sometimes distanced myself from, terrified. Orso, my stepson, who I felt was in some sort of danger by being with me. My stepson Orso, whose existence awakened me.

Orso was very young, but after the first or second summer at Sanary, I started to worry. A new conviction asserted itself: I had to speak.

I called Victor, terrified. 'I can't keep this quiet any longer, Victor. One day Orso will be the age you were then. Don't ask me to keep up a relationship with our parents rather than protecting this child.' I could feel my brother cleaving open and falling apart on the other end. I could tell he was getting angry. He too recognised this choice asserting itself. I could feel him confronting boundless fear. I could hear him begging me both to keep this quiet and to speak. And I realised that if I was the first to speak about our silences, his torment would assume a whole new reality. 'Keep this particular truth away from me, Camille, please.'

After more than ten years, I chose to speak. Not to everyone, of course. I told the man I loved. Probably using the wrong words. My mind wasn't ready, I didn't know how to formulate anything.

The Bistrot du Peintre, near the Place de la Bastille. A salad each. I couldn't breathe. I launched myself. I'd been keeping it to myself for years, I would lift the veil, I'd so longed for this. My body tensed, the prickle of sweat, my armpits were soaked. My voice croaked, I knew I was inaudible. I strained and strained: 'Thiago, about Sanary, I should tell you . . .' Should I give details? Tell him everything? Mention Victor, for sure. But what about me? Who would understand *that*?

Thiago knew my stepfather. He wasn't surprised. I talked to Thiago but I don't know what I expected of him. I talked to Thiago so he could protect his son, but hoping deep down that he wouldn't stop me seeing my mother.

Confronted with this contradictory plea, my boyfriend did what he could. Confronted with this double bind, he did his best. He spared me his questions.

★

We returned to Sanary, and my duality carved itself more deeply. Paralysed with fear, I started watching. I smiled but was constantly wary. I laughed, all the while fearing the worst. Most of all, I lied before a witness. For the first time, I was playing this role for real, demonstrating my permanent hypocrisy, forcing my despicable compromises on the situation, right in front of Thiago, before my lover's eyes. And I despised myself for it.

For all those years I'd put a brave face on it and laughed, but at my personal expense. Months of pulmonary embolisms. An autoimmune disease? A self-poisoned body.

★

This time Victor left for Chicago. For a year, with his wife, Alice, a childhood friend of ours. He called me in the evenings, 'Évelyne tells me you're dying, Camille, I should come back. But while your lungs are clogging up, mine are full of infection. I have pneumonia. The doctors have refused to let me travel. Wait for me, promise me.'

'Don't be frightened, brother, don't worry.'

Bernard was there. Colin too, though I couldn't talk to him.

My mother was tearful. I overheard her talking about herself on the phone. She brought me so many cakes in the hospital that I didn't know where to store them. I held my breath every time the door opened, terrified she would bring my stepfather.

Luckily, Thiago was playful: 'Your embolisms have embellished you. Camille and her pulmonary embellishments . . .'

★

Thirty-eight kilos and blocked arteries. What on earth could be wrong with this young woman?

She couldn't breathe.

Dominique, my saviour, my pulmonologist, who headed up the unit, said, 'You're very tired, Camille. I don't know what's going on with you but it's bad, I can see that. You need to listen to yourself now.'

If you only knew, Dominique . . .

There was nothing wrong with my lungs, Dominique. At most a snakebite. The thing hadn't stopped torturing me since I was fourteen. A monster that lived inside me and reared its head as soon as I thought I could catch my breath. A hydra that spread out its assaults over time, but its venom never managed to dissolve that primary poison. Its venom accumulated; its bites weren't successive, they were cumulative. And even though I was happy with Thiago, I didn't know how to drive it out.

If you only knew, Dominique . . .

Since I'd been with Thiago, the hydra had danced all the more furiously. I was now so happy, and I already hated myself for it. My guilt for that happiness battled it out with the guilt of having failed to stop anything.

If you only knew, Dominique . . .

My lungs would recover, but thanks to that unhoped-for love, the past was gate-crashing the present. Soon it would obliterate our future. My fear of allowing my own fragility to grow, my anger at being permanently absent from my own life, and sometimes my guilt for existing in the first place – they would all poison my life and my boyfriend's.

If you only knew, Dominique . . .

The hydra's faces had proliferated since I was fourteen. Stratifications and accumulations. A slow development that never eroded.

★

Months of sickness, trips to the hospital and suffocation.

I finished my thesis and dedicated it to Thiago. To him and to the future. Which was already inside my belly.

When the time came for the minister's daughter to have her thesis defence: 'Will he be here? Do you know if he'll be coming?' The French people's favourite 'personality' versus my seven years of toil on the concept of opposability – I wasn't up to it. Too tired. I didn't tell my father the date. I was too afraid of an awkward situation.

Of course, Victor was there, and I prayed my stepfather wouldn't come. And yet, deep down . . .

My Ph.D advisor announced that I had unanimously passed my defence, and I was now a doctor. Shame my father didn't see it.

The celebratory drink afterwards had to compete with my mother and her aura. The jury were stunned by Professor Pisier. I hadn't anticipated that one. Luckily, Thiago managed to keep his perspective, 'C'mon, better to laugh about it, let's sneak out so no one notices. As that song by Aragon goes, people live like this sometimes.' It was a shame for her, and for me.

Soon after that, Thiago and I had a daughter, with a full head of hair and plenty of colour. Lily, my beauty. An arrow, to quote her father.

'You're in labour,' Maya told me. 'I can see you are. My hand on your stomach thinks that's what this is.' I thought this funny: 'No, but seriously, it's a bit soon.' Thiago, with his experience, said I should relax and watch a DVD: '*To Our Loves.* Come on, we have time to watch it.'

By the end of the film the contractions were very close together. Thiago laughed and took me to the maternity unit.

Now I had to give birth to a baby whose sex we didn't know, a baby that hadn't turned. Arrangements were made for a Caesarean. On our side of the sheet separating us from the obstetrician, I listened to Thiago's words. A moment of intimacy for all eternity. For a few minutes I was in the real world.

Thiago's mother came to the maternity ward and sang, 'She so loved liberty, Lily, she dreamed of fraternity, Lily . . .' Lily, my lily of the valley.

★

Évelyne and Marie-France turned up at my bedside, overexcited and trying frantically to open the window so they could smoke. Marie-France was highly amused: 'Stupid fucking hygiene rules! Please don't tell me you'll ask me to wash my hands every time I come near your daughter?! She's so beautiful! She'll be a little Tanagra, like you! A Lili Brik, obviously!'

My mother fumed when the midwife handed me my baby to breastfeed her. And, naturally, she expressed her anger by asking simple questions – never attack freedom head-on. 'You're breastfeeding? Why? Did they make you? Aren't you scared of losing your freedom? Is this because it's natural? Nature's a convenient excuse when it comes to shutting women away, you know that . . .'

I just laughed: 'You and Thiago agree on this. But in

his case it's because he thinks it's disgusting. The pair of you can dress it up however you like, you can choose your excuses to hide the fact that you refuse to share me. I loved being pregnant and I love breastfeeding. Don't worry, there's nothing ideological about it, just a declaration of love to freedom. *My* freedom in this instance.' 'What freedom?' my mother yelled. 'Freedom means being able to choose not to take care of her. She's so adorable! Let's hope she's not a moron!'

Victor came, of course. And melted. I swear to you, seeing your twin's baby is something else.

No time to ease up. I'd only just given birth when I was made a lecturer in law, and had to scour the whole of France to secure a job in a university law faculty.

My baby was three weeks old, and I could hardly walk. I needed to go to Amiens, but couldn't leave Lily. 'Never mind!' Thiago said supportively. 'All three of us will go. You can work on your presentation when she's asleep. No way is your daughter going to be your punishment.'

We rented a car, arrived at the university. Selection committee, candidates in the corridor. Jostling for position without acknowledging it, aided and abetted by who we knew. I was there with my lover and my baby. I breastfed her in the corridor. I knew that my mother, so many miles away, would be appalled, her brand of feminism in tatters.

My name was called: 'Mademoiselle Kouchner . . .' Idiotic smile. An urge to destroy everything. 'Take her, Thiago, it's my turn!'

Operation successful. First university appointment.

*

Later I would drop Lily at nursery and run to catch my train to Amiens, leaving early in the morning and returning the same day. Impossible to stay away too long. Those were exhausting years.

My mother didn't help me. She didn't dare look after Lily. And anyway, how could I entrust her to her?

She sometimes came to pick her up from nursery, but always with me. A grandmother who refused to be left alone with her granddaughter. 'We all have our own ways, you know, I don't want to mess everything around. And isn't her daddy here? Women had to fight, remember? And all for this?' 'Do you go to her the minute she cries? Do you give her a bath every evening? Isn't there someone else who can look after her?'

My mother sat herself at the table in the living room. 'Some red wine? You must have a little glass for your mum. Viouli would love to come, but what with the radio and everything, he's very busy. I promised him I'd take some photos for him. He thinks she's so cute and blue-eyed.'

Uncorking wine, pouring a glass, drying my daughter after her bath, making dinner, soothing her, thinking about my seminars the next day . . . under my mother's spellbound and horrified eyes.

I would sometimes sit down with Évelyne just long enough to do the scratch cards she'd brought with her. Sometimes, thanks to those moments, I was Lily's mother and also Évelyne's daughter again. I savoured that happiness and would remember it.

When my mother came to see my daughter, I became her baby once more. I stroked her skin and drew strength from the gentleness in her eyes. I experienced her depth again. I felt protected and proud once more. With a smile, I was reunited with my beloved Évelyne. The one from before, the since-forever one. The one that some part of me couldn't bear to see change and could never abandon. My mummy. The best in the world.

Deep in the heart of me I hope that, for Lily, I'll have all her good qualities.

★

'Will you bring her to me in Sanary, my Camillou? I'll take a nanny with me, and you can leave her there with us.'

My heart was torn in two.

Through my own child I remembered. I remembered that I loved my mother absolutely. For my child's sake, I said nothing and tried to forget.

My father tried in his own way to accept being a grandfather.

Peals of laughter from Thiago when Bernard showed us around his new vacation house. Our daughter, aged two, ran all over the place. My father proudly caught her by the arm and hoisted her up off the floor. 'Look, all this is for you, my Juliette.' 'Bernard,' Thiago chuckled, 'better check with her mother, but I think her name's Lily.'

My father was a hero. I didn't have a choice, others had decided this for me. Even my mother absolved him when he became a minister in Nicolas Sarkozy's government. When I was a child, she'd made me recite these lines:

'When your illusion has lasted but a day, / Do not abuse that day when you speak of it.'

★

I rifled through my memories, drawing on my perspective as a child. Trying to untangle anger and admiration. Until I felt I had a split personality. My father exasperated me, but I loved him boundlessly. My mother was right.

My inner child's anger blew over, I took a deep breath and made some room for the admiration I felt for Bernard. I transformed his yelling fits and made them my allies, accepting that, in spite of everything, over and above his violence he loved me more than anything. Thanks to this respite, I thrived on the undiluted passion in his adoring expression and took refuge in this contradiction to sustain us, protect us and reunite us.

In my heart and my mind my father was unsurpassable. And I did realise that his rages were a part of his courage. Although he'd never explained this to me, he'd often demonstrated it.

The fact is, I finally believed in the honesty of his past battles. Striving for effective solutions, whatever the cost, and always having to be in the right place at the right time, including when he was under the spotlight – those were necessities. It was too easy to sit back, cross your arms, and judge.

Opting to stay silent was like running away: it showed a lack of courage. You can't save anyone without networks and cameras and speeches! Yelling louder than everyone else wasn't just self-centred, it was also extremely valiant, very brave.

I so wished I could do it.

★

Now, looking at Thiago, I understood my father better. Courage is the other side of the coin, strength armed with wonderment.

My father had this strength. Where plenty of others might have backed down out of cynicism or disillusion, my father had the power to put his faith in the beauty of things, to believe in it and to be furious if he saw it mistreated. He had that faith.

His anger derived from the mess he saw around him, from deterioration, suffering and the spring that never came. That was when my father would despair and grow angry. Stupidity, injustice, sickness and blighted childhoods turned his stomach. There was nothing calculated about it, it was simply insurrection.

My father had passed on to me his way of seeing the world. I would have preferred it to have been filtered through his tenderness rather than his anger, but what did it matter?

I moored myself to his gentleness whenever he deployed it, which he did in dribs and drabs, with no warning. Sometimes in the middle of a meal he would stroke my arm and sing: 'Is this how people live?' 'Forget-me-nots and roses too, flowers that say a thing or two . . .' My father had taught me songs ever since I was little. He knew every poem and recited the most beautiful verses. He said 'my girl' and wept over Victor Hugo's poem 'À Villequier', about his daughter Léopoldine, who drowned when she was nineteen. He said 'my girl' and tried to find in me the memories of all his past loves. My mother and the others, in spite of me.

And sometimes, without a moment's warning, my father laughed. He knew a thousand fables, a thousand stories. The same one recounted a hundred times. And I laughed to see him cry. Before, during and after the tale. He couldn't remember it at all. He wanted to tell me about his friend Robert's latest adventure, struggled to call it to mind, failed to but laughed anyway at the memory of it. The sheer ridiculousness of things and misinterpretations and misunderstandings, the sheer vanity of his memory. He gave up, took a deep breath, sometimes smoked, and became so kind.

With my silence, I was also protecting him.

A few months after Lily was born, Alice had a second son. As sometimes happened, Victor was 'absent'. Images, silences, thoughts. He called me and I did my best to reassure him, but could see that he was in deep. And I could see Alice getting angry, pointlessly.

We were in middle school when they met. We'd hardly turned twelve, and Victor was talking about her already. Alice had a Spanish type of beauty, was astute and open, generous and anchored, and her parents had banned her from coming to Sanary.

Later, after high school, she stole my brother's heart and became my sister. A friend who did me good, who breathed life into me. A friend who gave me refuge when she herself wasn't poleaxed. A friend who could accommodate the close connection, maintain some reserve and keep us the right distance apart. Being a twin's wife was a full-time job!

We watched one another grow up, and I watched them love each other. I got carried away with her dreams, which made my brother's life better. I trusted her.

But now Alice was exhausted. She was dealing with a second baby and an elusive husband. She told me she was going to leave him, she couldn't cope any more. I told Victor that he owed her the truth.

My brother was against it, but he opened up. He told his wife what had happened to him and what we'd been living with ever since.

And Alice – who'd seen nothing and noticed nothing – was angry with me. Most likely it was the shock. This man she'd known in junior high, this man she'd lived with for years, had hidden everything from her. But the recrimination was directed at me: Alice deemed me responsible: my silence was guilty. I was the one she resented. Not for long, but still . . .

Victor was annoyed with me too: 'I warned you, no one understands. Now Alice wants me to talk to Évelyne. Now the pair of you will be a fucking pain . . . It's really not that complicated: I don't want to talk about it. That's what works for me to build my life. I put my energy into other things. Why are you so set on stirring up the past? I need to get away, to focus on my work and my children. I need to move forwards, not stagnate in doom and gloom.'

I was angry with myself for a long time. He was right: it was his life, not mine. What was I doing interfering?

★

Alice had faith in Évelyne. Alice also believed that our parents would protect us. I think she was lucky to have been raised in a family where you could trust your mother.

She agreed to return to Sanary and made an arrangement with Victor: he would work all day and come home late in the evening. That meant he could mark out his own path, choose his own trajectory. He could be away while Évelyne was with her grandchildren.

Alice decided to return to Sanary, hoping Victor would feel supported, helped, protected. She took her boys to my mother; she did it for him, for them and for herself too. She thought it was obvious: Évelyne would leave my stepfather as soon as she knew. Alice had every intention of helping us talk to Évelyne.

We moved into the Farm while my mother and stepfather were in the Red House. Thiago had banned his son from going, with claims of alcoholism and other excesses typical of old arseholes. Orso was only ten, and I thought my stepfather was interested in teenagers, but I could see the way he looked at Orso, and I loathed him. Orso could probably feel it too. He always tried to get away from him, never laughed at his provocations, and clung to his father whenever my stepfather came near him.

We only ever saw my mother by the pool during the day, surrounded by happy children. Lily and her cousins played in the paddling pool and watered the garden with their 'Mamilyne'. Évelyne adored her grandchildren, thinking them the most beautiful, engaging children in the world. She melted with every look they gave her.

Évelyne was like my mother that summer. She was gentle, poised and calm. She was so happy.

We spent the rest of our time avoiding my stepfather. My heart exploded with stress as soon as he appeared. Alice would ask me to go to the pool ahead of her to be sure she wouldn't see him. She was having a crash course in the duality, the horrible hypocrisy we'd forced on ourselves. I think my stepfather quickly realised that she knew. Alice made no compromises with her loathing and anger. She made no compromises with my brother's love. Her dark eyes expressed her feelings perfectly clearly. I could see that with just a look she could protect her sons, settle her scores and silently let my stepfather know that his peaceful days were numbered.

I was petrified. The moment he came near me, I froze. I smiled and giggled on autopilot, but clutched Lily tightly in my arms. No way was he coming near her or touching her. No way would he tarnish her or even have the right to smile at her.

Alice and I were mothers, and we were in collusion. Everything was about to change.

That was fifteen years ago. It was our last summer all together at Sanary, but we didn't know it yet.

*

The following year, Colin decided to send his son to spend a few days with our mother. Colin wanted to send his two-and-a-half-year-old son to Sanary alone.

In those circumstances there was no room left for doubt. Victor immediately saw the urgency of the situation.

He went to see our brother and said, 'Don't send your son there. I'm going to tell you about something.' Colin was furious.

Then he remembered. And wasn't so very surprised. The stepfather who sometimes visited him in his bedroom on rue Joseph-Bara. The stepfather who came and measured his penis with a ruler the minute my mother's back was turned . . . Colin's memories resurfaced.

His son didn't go to Sanary and Colin was angry . . . with me, his sister. Like Alice, initially. 'Why didn't you say anything? My own sister, you betrayed me!'

★

Silence insinuated itself so softly between Colin and me. He hadn't noticed a thing. I'd done everything right. Just when the whole hellish thing had started, he'd gone off to live in his studio. We'd stopped listening to songs together in the evenings. We no longer had opportunities to talk to each other. Of course, he'd still been happy when he came home for dinner, and I'd been so thrilled to see him there, but I'd never been able to talk to him. I was terrified: The snake had already started its dance inside me.

When Colin had then left for Texas, I'd written a thousand times that I loved him. All in all, there isn't anything to add to that.

Colin now resented me and was threatening to reveal everything to my mother. Victor blamed me for this.

For Colin, learning a secret like that at the age of forty made his whole life feel like a lie. As if there hadn't been a jot of truth in his past. It meant losing the mother he adored in one fell swoop. It meant losing the story he'd told himself, his roots and his choices. All of it was untrue.

He was sad, and exasperated too. He explained that, now that there were three of us, the rules had changed, and it was unthinkable for him, as an adult, to pretend not to know. He said he would never see our stepfather again and was adamant that we should tell our father.

Anxious as well as relieved, I tried to explain to Colin that Victor wasn't ready, and we really needed to look out for him. I didn't say anything about myself. Or anything about the hydra that so terrified me.

Colin gradually understood. He wouldn't say anything, he would keep it to himself if that was what Victor wanted, but he would keep trying to get Victor himself to speak. Meanwhile, with me, he chose to be suspicious.

★

How could we handle this so that my mother suspected nothing? How could we ensure that my mother continued to be a grandmother?

I returned to Sanary with Thiago but without my brothers in 2007, I think. Perhaps it was 2008.

My memory's failing. Certain years are completely erased, and I'll never get them back. I think that, once he was in the know, Colin joined us somewhere else in July. We talked, we tried to clear the air.

Colin didn't go to Sanary that summer, he didn't know how to look at my mother.

Victor didn't go either. I don't remember why. Probably because Alice quietly understood that he wouldn't talk to our mother, and it made her very angry.

My mother couldn't understand why her sons refused to go to Sanary.

So I went there alone that summer. 'You go to Sanary,' Victor had told me. 'Tell Évelyne it's not that I don't love her. Whatever you do, don't say anything. Go to Sanary and reassure her . . . I'd go if I could . . .' I agreed to that, but never succeeded in consoling my mother.

Between two classes at the start of the new academic year, my backside freezing, I peed onto a little stick. I was pregnant with a second baby. Thiago, I'm pregnant and I love you alone. I want to live in your detachment and with your talent. I want joy more than my strong will; I want our children and a horizon.

Like with Lily, nine months of happiness and nine months of pain. Gynaecology and pulmonology. Injections every day, successive scans. My bouts of pulmonary embolism left behind. Injection, nursery, Amiens, nursery, bath, dinner, injection. A story at bedtime, getting back up, singing. A glass of wine for my mother, then a second and a third.

Really need to prepare my seminars. And what about my exams?

*

We had a son. A blazing sun.

My Nathan, a prophet in our country. Blond, like my brother. Strong, like his father.

My Nathan, with eyes 'so deep my memories get lost in them'.

My Nathan, with such blue eyes like Évelyne, and Victor.

We had a son whom Thiago wanted to call Georges, forgetting my grandfather, who took his own life. We had a son, and I understood at last. My thoughts dispersed and then gathered together. We had a son, and I was flooded with immeasurable disgust.

With that baby in my belly, I already knew. I knew we had to avoid everything. I knew that Sanary was over, and I would never go there again. Never again would I see that house from my childhood, the one I'd been visiting for thirty years. Never again that refuge and the heat of summer. Never again the laughter, the French tarot and the wit. Never again the smell of thyme on my hands. Peeing out of doors with my mother. Never again Évelyne's smile among the mimosa flowers, our games of Scrabble by the pool, lying on our stomachs. Never again the pines and olive trees.

I insisted that Victor tell my mother. I explained again and again why it would be impossible for my son to have any contact with our stepfather, and that he – Victor – must stop asking me to go there. And, for the first time, I said, 'If you don't say anything, then I will.'

Colin and Alice helped me, also trying to persuade Victor: 'Tell her what happened. Tell her that incest isn't a freedom. Tell her about this wound you've carried since you were a boy.'

Victor may not have been ready, but he did it.

My memories are out of their depth again.

I feel as if it was the day Nathan was born, the day I was delivered, that my brother told Évelyne everything. He finally told her the truth. He told her what her husband subjected him to over several years. He told her that he'd kept quiet to protect her. He told her that I'd always known.

Breathing. Getting up. Episiotomy. Backache. Getting up. Breathing. Welcoming my baby. Feeding him. Rocking him. Bathing him. Suckling him. Getting up. Breathing. Not forgetting the blood that's still flowing, the tears tumbling down. It was hormonal. Not sleeping. Jaundice. UV treatment. We stayed a little longer. Getting Thiago to come over with the children.

Thiago's whole family at the maternity ward. Smiling. Being so happy. Saying how wonderful it was.

With my heart ripped out. My heart in my mouth. Wanting to throw up. The hydra was refining its characteristics. The harrowing fear. The overwhelming fear that they would all take their own lives. My brother, my little brother, my twin. I'm sorry, forgive me, I didn't want to force you. Will you be okay? Will you have the heart to come and see my baby?

Victor called me: 'There, it's done, I told her everything. Congratulations on the baby. Évelyne didn't say anything. She left. Marie-France took her in.'

★

Two days later, my mother came to the maternity ward. Two days later, my mother, covered in bruises. Devastation written all over her face. She said that she'd fallen on a train platform, then she stopped talking.

I told her to pick Nathan up, she wouldn't look at me. She sat down as far away from me as she could and refused to speak to me.

My milk coming in. Évelyne like a ghost. A spectre of a mother. Nathan not making a sound. A mesmerising silence punctuating his wailing. I was horrified by the state Évelyne was in, and this time Marie-France wasn't there. But she would come to see me later, for once without her sister.

★

The end of 2008. The end of secrecy. At the end of 2008 the world fell apart.

Almost immediately the weight started falling off me, my body shrank and shrank and disappeared.

The midwife was amazed. Physical therapy for my perineum in an uncomfortable position, my intimacy defiled. Her hand in my vagina. 'Tell me about your baby, your house, how happy you were when he was delivered, you must rest, hand the baby over to his daddy, you know you should, times have changed, he must take care of him. He's not here, well, of course he isn't, they're all the same! He doesn't know how to, but he'll learn. Ask your mother, ask the grandparents. You must learn to trust them with him. Tell me why you chose his name, tell me about the best days of your life, your most cherished memory.'

And lying there with my legs spread, with Nathan in

his car seat next to me in this consulting room where happiness was usually welcomed in, I said nothing. I was burning inside. 'My mother, of course. His grandparents, naturally . . .' Shut up and get your fingers out!

Marie-France noticed me shrinking too. 'You've gone too far now, Camille. Are you doing a crazy supermodel number on us or something?! You have to stop.' She came to see Nathan and gave me a red cashmere sweater with a zipper and a hood for when I was breastfeeding. A sweater from the market in Sanary, the sweater that Lily still wears to this day. She smiled at me: 'Your mother's a coward. Talk to your father.'

Marie-France, my aunt, a pillar in the middle of this storm.

My mother's silence, my brother's silence. I was in despair. Is this what it's like when you find your voice again?

A year went by, and I was at home alone. Sanary was over. Who I had been, over too. Roots, memories, connections, all over.

I took care of my children and took a competitive exam to secure work in Paris. Putting a brave face on it, being the best, the one they'd choose.

A year went by, and my mother hardly visited. A year went by, and because Évelyne now knew, Alice refused to see her. A year went by, and Victor couldn't breathe. Nothing happened even though a whole year had happened.

My brother occasionally had phone calls from my mother. She told Victor that our stepfather didn't deny it. 'He's sorry, you know. He tortures himself about it constantly. But he's thought about it, and you clearly must have been more than fifteen. And there wasn't any sodomy. I mean fellatio really is very different.'

She said more accusatory things to me: 'How could you betray me like that? Starting with you, Camille, my daughter, you should have told me. I could see how much you all loved my man. I always knew you'd try to steal him from me. I'm the victim here.'

Apart from that, she tried to silence me. She asked if I'd like to write a guidebook on the collection she was curating, sent me a little something to supplement my income, told me she loved me and was lonely, so far from her children and grandchildren. Apart from that, hardly another word.

I spent years trying to please her and reconnect with her.

As a boy, my brother had warned me: 'You wait, they'll believe me but they won't give a damn.' Shit. He was right.

★

Okay, if they didn't understand, we'd just have to explain it to them.

I'm going to explain this to you, you whose rhetoric

fills the airwaves, you who influence students with your analyses and who swagger on television.

I'm going to explain that you could at least have apologised. Shown some acknowledgement and concern.

I'm going to remind you that, instead, you threatened me. The message on my answering machine: 'I'm going to kill myself.'

I'm going to explain to you, you who call us your children. When a teenager says yes to the man raising him, that's incest. He said yes at an age when his own urges were emerging. He said yes because he trusted you and your fucked-up apprenticeship. And the real act of violence was your decision to exploit this, do you get that? Because the truth is that in that moment, the boy wouldn't have been able to say no to you. He would have been too eager to please you and find out about all this.

I'm going to explain to you that from then on, when it kept happening, the boy would say yes to avoid acknowledging the full horror of the situation. It would keep happening and he would blame himself, he'd think it was his fault and that he'd had it coming to him. And that would be your triumph, your escape route.

Georges and Paula dead by suicide, Évelyne in despair,

Bernard never around, you got lucky with us being so lost and needy . . .

But when the hydra sleeps, I become aware of all this, and I don't forget.

I don't forget the sort of couple you were. Sartre and Beauvoir? Only the *familia grande* believed that.

The two of you in unison rammed the lessons home: Michel Foucault and punishment. Never inform on anyone, never condemn anyone in this society where there's always punishment in store. Know how to adapt, be flexible and hope for rehabilitation. Be wary of the law.

Which brings me to my law degree: rape entails any act of sexual penetration, whatever kind it may be, committed using violence, coercion, threats or an element of surprise. Well, that was one hell of a surprise!

And what about coercion? The fucking moral pressure involved! Like the fact that we loved you so much, do you see? Like the fact that we trusted you so completely and would have defended you to the death if necessary! Like the fact that we couldn't even send you to prison because we were so afraid for you. Like the fact that it was *you*. Not someone else. *You*.

You, who assaulted my brother for months, do you see

the problem? *You* did it practically in front of me, and you didn't give a damn, making me an accomplice to your interference. Are you starting to see the terrors that have been haunting us ever since?

Let's be clear about this:

Article 222-24 of the French Criminal Code

Rape is punished by twenty years' criminal imprisonment . . .

4° where it is committed by a legitimate, natural or adoptive ascendant, or by any other person having authority over the victim . . .

Article 222-31-1 of the French Criminal Code

Rape and sexual assaults are classified as incestuous when committed by:

1° an ascendant;

2° a brother, a sister, an uncle, an aunt, a nephew or a niece;

3° or any other person, including a partner or family member, having legal or de facto control over the victim.

But you're a professor of law too. You're a lawyer. You know perfectly well that, because of the statute of limitations, you'll get out of this. Everything's fine for you.

Twenty years. Otherwise, it would be twenty years.

Years went by steeped in silence from the Sanaryans. Only Marie-France fought.

★

When Nathan was born and my mother sought out her sister to bemoan her fate, when she told her, 'If only Camille had said something sooner, I could have left him. It's too late now. I no longer have that freedom,' Marie-France begged her. And if it had been a question of money, she'd have given her some. 'You're not alone, leave! I'm here.'

Marie-France threw herself doggedly into this undertaking. She did what she could to battle the horror. She told her friends that her sister was with a paedophile who'd picked on her son. It was unbearable, unacceptable.

For months she tried to find ways to sway my mother, to open her eyes and persuade her to leave him.

The microcosm of powerful people at Saint-Germain-des-Prés were very soon informed. Many of them knew, and most behaved as if it was of no concern. A few commented, 'Well, surely what's really despicable about the whole thing is that it was homosexual?' One child from the *familia grande* reported back his parents' reaction: 'Incest isn't right. But howling with the rest of the pack is absolutely not right!' What pack?

★

The Sanaryans, the *familia grande*, disappeared; very few of them spoke to us again. And there I was desperately hoping Victor was wrong. There I was hoping they would convince our parents not to turn the tables. I hadn't anticipated that my stepfather would try to clear his name by dressing it up as a relationship and blaming it on my brother, and that some of them would believe him. Women mostly – talk about *précieuses ridicules*! What cruel women.

Meanwhile, Marie-France was in despair. The sisters had fallen out for the first time. Really fallen out: they'd stopped talking to each other. Marie-France sometimes came back to my mother, but she was met with only silence and cruelty.

*

The house in the Basque Country, Thiago's family home, was now my refuge. It was cold, damp and not sunny enough for me, but I loved the smell of it. I loved the sense of calm and the cool sheets. I always loved being reunited with my mother-in-law and seeing my children there.

Morning light, coffee percolating. I was about to take a cup to Thiago. 'It's my turn, for once.' Being back in his arms, a medley of sweet nothings, the radio on, France Inter, 24 April 2011.

My phone in my hand, I was waiting for my cup to fill. Vibrations. First smoke of the day. My eyes on my phone. Vibrations. *Le Monde*'s banner headline: 'Actress Marie-France Pisier Dead.' My heart stopped.

Vibrations. Colin was calling me. 'What the hell is this?' 'I don't know, it must be a mistake.' I couldn't breathe.

More vibrations. And again. All at once masses of calls. The *familia* that had kept so quiet suddenly wanted to know. From me. Even with their newfound courage, they didn't yet dare call my mother. And in my blindness, I saw their names pop up. Everything was muffled, my brain paralysed.

But Thiago came running down the stairs. Thiago's eyes on mine, the way he looked at me, I instantly succumbed to the truth of it.

As he rarely did, Thiago put his arms around me. As never again and never before, Thiago was with me and I understood. I recognised that moment. The moment like a dull thud struck for all eternity, a moment that silently altered reality. That moment was happening again.

Letting Timothée know before the media descended on him. Waiting a while before waking Rose in Mexico. Timothée and Rose, my dear cousins, now abandoned in this family of lunatics. My cousins, who'd purged themselves of my stepfather as soon as they knew. My cousins, who were damaged for ever.

The hydra's heads spread out slowly and coiled tightly around my neck. The silence was enormous. I walked away from the brewing coffee and from Thiago's arms. I called my mother. I dialled her number, shaking. My mother, I knew this, would never recover. Her sister's death. Like that. When they'd fallen out. I'd have preferred being forced to howl for all eternity than confront the pain to come. I'd rather have died than have to bear this new guilt.

Évelyne picked up. Her voice, the voice of my mum who was now lost for ever: 'It's kind of you to call, my baby. Last night. They found her . . . Like the others, she did it too, she killed herself.'

Part
IV

Major-league criminal lawyers. Heavyweights of the bar. I choose them deliberately. The ones who head up the list of the best firms. Well, we have to try to counterbalance things. We have to try to match up to my stepfather's and my mother's reputations, the great professors of law. We have to ready ourselves to counter their friends' potential denials, some of them top lawyers themselves, now compelled to defend their own silence.

Now that Évelyne has died, Colin, Victor and I arrange a meeting with lawyers. We tell them what happened and describe the context too. We try not to leave anything out. The partner takes her time and asks Victor for exact details. She asks us to try to tell her who knew, and since when. She then arranges another meeting a few days later so that she can work on the file.

★

On the appointed day, my brothers and I meet at a café just downstairs from the lawyer's office. We chat about our children and then go up. Climbing the stairs, it occurs to me that it's strange how scared I feel whenever I come near people in the legal profession.

The lawyers are there waiting for us.

Large glass table. We all sit down. We can start.

Using frank words, her voice measured, the senior partner speaks first: 'Before we start, I want to dispel any ambiguity.' She turns to Victor, her voice filling the entire room: 'You were the victim of a crime, sir. I listened to what you told me, and this case is very clear. I've found other cases with the same context, the same ages and the same events, where the stepfather was given a substantial sentence. You were a victim of incest, sir. And it doesn't matter that he's trying to say you made no attempt to resist him. It doesn't matter that he's trying to say you were older. It's always the same in all these cases. In my view, your stepfather is guilty and should be in prison.'

I stop breathing. My whole body is taut. Even the hydra, which has started dancing, is suspended in the air, completely paralysed. Apart from the senior partner's words, the silence in the room is deafening.

I can't move. Or just my eyes can. I look around the room: lawyers, Colin, lawyers, Colin. I hardly dare look at Victor. I wish I could take him in my arms though.

The words, these words that Victor is hearing.

The words, these words that I never stopped searching for in my years of legal work, but until now, they've never been enough.

The words, these words I was waiting to hear. I'm no longer the only one saying them. This simple legal classification. Not a moral judgement. An offence. A crime punishable by law.

This recognition of the suffering. From a third party at last.

A torrent of tears is in full spate inside me, a torrent that the hydra has kept replenishing since I was fourteen. I can hear it coursing wildly inside.

I turn to Colin, wanting to see him hear the same words as me. I want to watch as, in a flash, things become perfectly clear for Colin too.

The words, these words coming thirty years later; I hope they will foster Victor's determination, and finally convince him he has the right to complain.

The lawyer is looking at my twin alone. I can see what's going to happen.

'Crimes of this nature can currently be taken to court up to thirty years after reaching majority. We now have until the victim turns forty-eight to press charges, so you could do it, but the law is not retroactive. It applies only to victims who have been raped more recently. Like a lot of other children, you've taken a long time to speak out. It's only natural. Denouncing someone close to you is even more difficult, and you probably needed to wait until your mother died . . . But it's too late. Or, to be more precise, the crime was committed too long ago. The law doesn't differentiate between the rape of minors and incest in terms of its dictates. There's nothing that can be done to him now. I'm so sorry.'

'You must speak to your father, my Tanagra,' Marie-France told me before she died. 'I want him to know. Your mother may not be doing anything, but your father will.' Marie-France trusted him to protect us. She said, 'Talk to your father, Camille, or I'll do it.'

She didn't have time to.

★

What happened to her?

Found dead, wedged in a chair at the bottom of her swimming pool. Cicadas and mimosa. Thyme and rosemary. The dog didn't bark . . . In real life. For real. In this reality.

I remember that evening in April 2011 when Victor

and I went out for dinner together. Two days before Marie-France's funeral. I'd just returned from the Basque Country, and as we always do in the toughest of times, we met up. At La Sardine on the place Sainte-Marthe, in my neighbourhood.

This time the uppercut to the solar plexus had completely winded us. We were absolutely incapable of crying. We looked at each other and spoke words released one after the other into the silence. We were poleaxed, wild-eyed, devastated. 'She can't have done this to us, surely?' 'They can't have done this to us!' 'Do you think it's our fault?' 'A nightmare.' 'Without Marie-France, things are going to get complicated now.' 'And what will happen to mum?'

*

Marie-France didn't have time to tell my father. But thanks to the inquest, her computer was searched. Her email exchanges with my mother must have been found. Victor was summoned by the juvenile squad. A friend of Marie-France's had confirmed that 'Yes, yes, what they're saying is true. The stepfather even acknowledges it. He interfered with Victor when he was a teenager. That's why the sisters fell out.'

My brother came to join me at the law courts. I was shaking from defending a case; he'd just seen the police and was clutching his statement.

'Wait, I'll read it to you. Do you think it's good? Do you remember?' Nightmare. 'I told the cops to be discreet. I don't give a damn what could happen to him but I don't want to fuck up the life I've built, my work, my children, my whole life! Surely they won't sling all that in the papers! I hope they won't be a pain in the arse to Luz and Pablo. And what about Évelyne?'

The concourse at the law courts. We sat on a bench.

My brother made me read the statement he'd had to make. All the details. Everything. Those words right in front of me, those bald, harsh words. Those words describing images that had traumatised me as a child.

I read it and my memory was instantly diluted. The questions selected by the inquiry came at me out of the dark. 'Who?' 'When?' 'Where?' 'How many times?' 'Did he force you?'

Like my brother, I remembered everything, but also

nothing. How old were we exactly? How many times did he do it? 'Who?' That I did know. 'When?' More or less. 'Where?' Pretty much everywhere. 'How many times?' No idea. 'Did you try to resist him?' No, not physically.

I read it and immediately pictured my stepfather. I read it and was terrified. Not of what had already happened but of what could happen. The details were clear, there was no room for discussion. The police even reminded Victor, 'Of course you didn't fight him. That's always the way. That doesn't alter the fact that he was the adult, and what's more your stepfather, and he had no right to. Still, let us remind him of that.'

Prison! My heart pounded ludicrously fast. I could see the same terror on Victor's face. Once again, that feeling that we were the cause of some colossal mistake. Once again, we anticipated the disaster this might produce. Once again, we were terrified children. No! Too scary! It's just too scary! It'll hurt the people we love. We can't do this to them. Not send him to prison. We've been taught how to behave, we're not like that. The hydra eyed me. The past couldn't be altered.

I took my brother's hand, but he withdrew it

straightaway. He didn't want any commiseration from me. Neither did he want to see the fear in my eyes.

I took this to mean: 'No. I do not want to press charges. This matter is none of your business.' Everything blurred. Profound relief and huge disappointment. The hydra unleashed its rage.

★

The inquiry was stopped. I had that account of incest before my eyes and the inquiry was stopped. Police everywhere, justice nowhere. No need to remind me of that.

Still, one of the police tried to toot his own horn. Journalists were tipped off. Phone calls, vibrations, phone calls, vibrations. Our parents in Sanary were warned first, and instantly judged us: 'Bastards! You leaked the whole thing.' And we replied, stunned, 'Not at all, mum, Victor was summoned. He didn't ask for any of this.' My mother's voice on the phone condemned us all over again: 'I hate your perversity. Everyone's going to know about this now.' I told Victor about this, and his immediate response was: 'Luz and Pablo need to know. They really need to be told before this gets out.' Victor was insistent with our mother: 'It's their father's job to tell them.'

I tried to explain to Nathan and Lily why I cried so much. 'Marie-France has died. It's come as a shock. I can't tell you how it happened.' What I was mostly thinking was that if the journalists were persistent, my father was the one who really needed warning.

★

Victor called me one morning: 'You and Colin should be happy, I really have to tell him now.' And then his tone softened: 'Okay then, here goes.' He called back an hour later: 'It's done. I'm off for a walk. I don't feel like talking right now.'

That same evening Bernard summoned me. That same evening Bernard frightened me. I was aware of his physical courage; he'd held his own all through his life. 'I'll smash his face in,' he'd told Colin. And the two of us shuddered at the prospect that he might actually do it.

I explained to Bernard that he needed to say nothing. I reiterated Victor's words and added a smattering of law: 'You'll end up going to prison, do you get that?' I used my father's own vocabulary and tried every avenue to convince him. 'We need to move forward. You always say no one should ever look back, Dad. Victor doesn't want to talk about this any more. We need to move forwards.'

And the one time he listened to me, I knew I'd regret it.

One of the last times I saw my mother was in 2011, at Marie-France's funeral in Sanary. A place associated with my stepfather and his cousin. A place associated with the husbands.

Her blue eyes hidden. Windproof sunglasses, stormproof sunglasses. Eye contact forbidden. Angry kisses. A half-hearted 'Hello' and a peck on each cheek. Chilling.

A half-hearted 'Hello,' but such extraordinary softness. The softness of her cheeks. Her smell. Sunshine and cigarettes. Just for a few moments I recognised my mother.

Thiago had booked us a hotel room, and we'd arrived the day before. The revelation meant we would never go back to the house. We had to disappear, to hide ourselves.

Alone. Like pariahs. Spending the night at a distance from my mother and my younger brother and sister, from the new iteration of the *familia grande*, even though they were all together.

I said a few words by the graveside, although I hadn't been invited to. Thiago had encouraged me to do it. Words scribbled on a notepad that same morning, expressing my pain, describing my aunt. Hoping my mother was watching and those who knew were listening.

Marie-France, the only one on our side. Marie-France, her beauty, intelligence and courage. Saying goodbye to her, first in New Caledonian: '*Tata*, my *tata* . . . you showed me that there's no love, there are just signs of love. I'll try to measure up.'

Jealous and furious, Évelyne quickly shut me down: 'You're making a fool of yourself, you shouldn't have said anything. Paula and Marie-France didn't love you. They had other things to think about . . . That's not what love is.'

*

Three years earlier my aunt had said 'Leave' and my mother had stayed. My aunt had said 'Speak out' and my mother had kept quiet.

And now my aunt was dead.

No pistol or pills this time. She was found wedged in a chair at the bottom of her swimming pool.

Marie-France died while my mother was telling me: 'Marie-France is crazy and you're to blame. If you'd spoken sooner, I could have left. Your silence is your responsibility. If you'd spoken, none of this would have happened.' And she added, 'There was no violence. Your brother was never forced. My husband did nothing wrong. Your brother's the one who betrayed me.'

*

After that pronouncement from my mother, my anger towards my parents and myself mushroomed. At last. The hydra started a new dance. I'd been such a fool! 'Your brother's the one who betrayed me'! Why did I ever think my mother would help me?

After that pronouncement from my mother, effortless happiness drained away. For a long time. I couldn't breathe, but my days started regardless. Every morning I knew I would constantly have to tackle the hydra and its abhorrent incarnations, my anger born of shame, my guilt, my sadness and my disgust at the truth. My day-to-day existence was contaminated. The slightest move I made cost me, and that was terrifying. Once I was away from Thiago's arms, one-on-ones were the worst part of the day: meeting a co-worker at the university, bumping into an acquaintance in the street, answering an unexpected question from a shopkeeper, taking the children to the doctor. Every exchange carved out an abyss. I was suffocating. Anything that needed me to be there was unlivable.

Whatever the circumstances, I was more comfortable running away. I could walk into a room full of people without daring to say hello. It was easier thinking no one could see me.

After that pronouncement from my mother, I stopped moving forwards. At university, I took part in my friends' teacher training seminars, I encouraged and congratulated them, but cut myself no slack. I stopped talking. There was no point in it, and I was tired. My girlfriends thought they were respecting my freedom: 'It doesn't matter, you always give the feeling you're somewhere else anyway.'

After Marie-France died, guilt – my twin sister – spread its wings. The wily creature hid and evolved and tried to stay out of reach. It assumed the form of excessive censoriousness, of pointless crippling nostalgia, of lacerating anger, of abortive intellectual rigour . . .

★

People around me, every component of my family, said nothing. Perhaps out of reticence, but also sometimes for want of courage. Uncles, cousins and reinvented friends only very occasionally tried to talk to my mother. There was no one to tell our parents to love us.

Only Muriel, Philippe and Fabienne came to see me once, and they openly condemned my stepfather in front of me. Dominique tried to persuade my mother to join us for the summer holiday. And I got the feeling that all those generations of Sanary children, headed up by Emmanuelle, were horribly embarrassed by their own parents' silence. I gathered that some people, mostly women, decided to stop working with my stepfather.

But apart from that, the *familia grande* went to ground. The old and new batches moved about like earthworms. There were murmurings, repeated words, but they never showed their faces or came to talk to me. People I'd trusted, people who'd more or less raised me, never came to ask about what had happened. I never saw them asking themselves questions and wondering whether they hadn't fucked up a bit too. There was no one trying to comfort us or tell us we shouldn't feel guilty.

Even after our mother died, their silence would be a prison to us.

★

Their silence wasn't just cowardice. Some of them were only too pleased to keep quiet about it – a duty that proved they belonged to the clique. It was an endlessly necessary, additional mark of their identity. Left-leaning and upper class, they also 'keep their dirty laundry at home'. Just like in the days of Madame de La Fayette, this close-knit society fed on every perversity, and it certainly didn't want to share. Even when there was a crime involved, and a crime against fourteen-year-old children at that. You had to be in on the secret to be accepted in this court, this *familia grande* that was busy scheming. Their children reported back some of the things they'd said. The *précieuses* asked, 'Who are we to judge? What bastards those children are! Hounding their mother like that. They won't let her see her grandchildren. Unbelievably cruel . . .'

Contrary to my expectations, they didn't see what I thought I knew as a responsibility. Quite the opposite! For the weakest of them, being privy to the facts was a new way to demonstrate their submissiveness to my stepfather, the most effective tool to show their allegiance to the sovereign, to swear loyalty to him. They definitely wouldn't be the ones to out this crime. Relatively recently, one of them told me anxiously, 'You have no idea! Dozens and dozens of people are in the know . . .' and I realised that he was defending his own turf.

Like with Poe and his purloined letter. Whoever is privy to the secret has newfound weight. Our misery was their power.

*

After Marie-France died, I understood more clearly why I could no longer walk along the Left Bank, through the streets of my childhood.

The hydra siphoned its energy from me, grew stronger and tortured me. I had no control over my heart and its frantic beating. I found it difficult just going out for lunch . . . I turned down parties, not that I was invited to many. I felt that danger lurked on every street corner. I slipped past like a ghost if I had to, and then would inexplicably start to run. Sometimes it would be because I'd seen my mother and stepfather, even though I desperately longed to go and hug them. Mostly because, since that pronouncement from my mother, all my glorious childhood memories had been torpedoed.

And deep inside my heart lay this truth: I avoided my old neighbourhood for fear that I wouldn't be able to stop loving my stepfather. I avoided my old neighbourhood because my stepfather never, ever spoke to me again.

The man I so needed in order to exist. I couldn't go back to the streets of my childhood because the brutal rift between us burned me and I was afraid that, if I saw him, my feelings would be ambivalent. I was afraid I wouldn't be brave enough to hate him and to demonstrate the fact.

After Marie-France died, I couldn't go back to the streets of my past because perversity had stolen them from me. Just as it had permanently robbed me of Sanary. I was forbidden a past. It's a terrible heartache being deprived of your childhood memories and the people you love.

After Marie-France's funeral, with the exception of a few spiteful emails, my mother never really talked to me again.

I did try, though. 'Mum, I can't agree with the way you live your life as a woman. You shouldn't stay with that man. But you're my mother and that's something I want to keep.' She refused everything. She abandoned Lily and barely laid eyes on Nathan. She never met Victor's daughter, and as her defence, she chose to tell her friends that it was we who had disowned her. We'd disowned her because we were ashamed of having betrayed her.

Until that message on 11 January, six years after Marie-France died.

I was having lunch with Maya. I didn't pick up. My mobile phone said 'Évelyne Pisier'. It knocked the breath out of me. 'Are you going to pick up?' 'No, no, I'll explain some day.'

On the way home I listened to her message: 'Hello, it's mum. It turns out I have lung cancer. I'd like you to let your father know.'

I'm reporting that message from memory. It's still on my voicemail but I can't listen to it. I just can't. I would hear my mother's voice, and for now I can't deal with it.

Four weeks later she was dead. Asphyxiated.

★

My mother called me on 11 January and she died on 9 February. Rather short. Rather quick. With my stepfather's help, the pulmonologist had persuaded her that she needed emergency surgery. Before the biopsy. Before they knew it was so serious.

31 January: my mother didn't cope well with the surgery. She must have suffered a great deal. She cried out as she came to, so they put her back to sleep. Eight days in an induced coma, while they tried to find the bacterium that had triggered her septic shock. They

didn't find anything. Septic shock all over again. Cardiac arrest. End of story.

During that period, I would call the hospital, and my sister – who was there – would relay the news.

My stepfather had left for Paris. Too tough for him to be there. Or perhaps he was too busy making radio shows. Until the surgeon ordered him to return: 'It's not looking good, you need to come back.' 'Yes, but he couldn't,' Luz told me. 'He couldn't bear to. Poor Daddy.'

Bernard piped up, 'She drinks so much, it's inescapable. She smokes like a chimney, she won't recover . . .' 'No, no, don't you worry. There's nothing you can do for her. Take your kids skiing. Don't ruin things for them.'

Being reunited with my stepfather, being anywhere near him, was unthinkable. I've never managed it. His physical presence is unbearable. He was meant to be at the hospital, and if he had been, he would have filled every corner of the place. Even with my mother sick, I wouldn't have been able to accept the idea of being around him.

★

I left with Victor, Alice and the children. I called Luz four times a day, every day. Sometimes she reassured me, sometimes she worried me. I tried to speak to the doctors, but was only allowed nurses. I relayed everything to my brothers.

I called my father to ask, 'Can you talk to the doctors because you're clearly qualified to?' Bernard was leaving for Madrid, but he would call back, that was a promise.

Not a word from the *familia grande*. Not one phone call. The *familia grande* had gone to ground and forgotten that we existed. 'Zazie's here,' Luz told me. I wasn't allowed any more information. I called. I called in vain.

Until that nurse on the morning of 9 February. I said I was her daughter, 'Yes, yes, honestly, another daughter.' The first one, the one that she used to love once upon a time.

'There's only an hour left, your mother's dying.'

Two weeks before the operation, Victor made me go down to the South. Two weeks before the operation, he didn't give me a choice. He came to collect me: 'I've bought your tickets. We're going to see mum. Now.' A done deal.

'We'll come to see you next weekend,' Victor had insisted to Évelyne. She said no. 'No, I'm too tired, I need my strength for the operation.' She made us call our father: 'Don't visit her,' he told us. 'It's the patient's prerogative. We must respect her wishes. I'm asking as a doctor that you don't disturb her.'

On that occasion, Victor refused. He took me with him.

We spent the night at a hotel in Marseille, then we went by car. We found a table at the café in Bandol and called our mother: 'We're here. We'll be here for the day. You can choose not to see us but we're here.'

An hour later my mother agreed: 'Half an hour. Fine, but just half an hour. I'm tired.'

We got back into the car. Beautiful January light. Sunshine. Sanary, in fact. Heading for the familiar shore that was our mother.

We parked the car at the entrance to the grounds. This place from our childhood, a place of happiness and violence. Marie-France was buried there, Marie-France was so near. Her hand in mine.

Évelyne appeared among the mimosas. Really tiny, so tiny. So pale. Huddled in her coat. My mother was permanently cold. And how she'd loved buying trashy clothes at the market in Sanary. With her sister. Sweaters in faux wool, but mostly rayon and comfortable little-old-lady shoes. Scarves of every kind, found all over the place, impregnated with Aromatics Elixir. True, they cost nothing, but when you bought that many . . .!

I tried to catch her eye. It was a mistake. 'I honestly wonder what you're doing here. I'm here with the man I love. I'm lucky. He's taking care of everything. I'm staying here. Don't come and see me.'

Turning my stomach. Leaving me totally empty. Knocking the breath out of me.

Victor sat down and said in a kindly voice, 'Of course we're here. You're going to have an operation. It's serious.'

Please, mum, don't let's pretend it isn't serious.

A letter

Darling Mum,
My Mamouchka,

I wake in the mornings and it's you I see. I talk
and it's you I hear. My skin is like yours. You're in
everything, everywhere. Omnipresent. And I love
you so much.

But, darling mum, my Mamouchka, who will
remember us now that you're not here? Who
will remember those years and bear witness?

Remember, mum: Victor so adored you,
he loved you even more than me. Remember,
Évelyne: he was blond and I was brunette. Victor
was short and I was tall. He was gentle and

focused, and I was lively and chaotic. Most of all remember: we were your children.

Victor is my twin. He's not my doppelgänger. He's not my friend. He's not my lover. He's your son and I love him more than anyone. Victor isn't me. That's just how it is.

He asked me to, but I didn't protect him. I didn't know how to.

Because until you died, mum, Victor and I were moulded into one. I didn't feel any difference. What he wanted was what I wanted. His wishes all muddled up with mine, inseparably, inextricably, and yet deep down they were already very different.

It's true, mum, my brother told me to say nothing, and until today I have. But my silence wasn't because of my promise. Whatever you may believe, there's no pact, no sworn secret. My silence is a product of the beliefs held by the child I once was. My silence is the result of your breakdown and the lack of trust at home, mum. After Paula took her own life.

We were so young, and you adults seemed so big and important and vital to us. How could our stepfather want anything but what was best for us? Who was I to oppose it? Who would have killed themselves then?

It's parents who make their children keep these things quiet. Not brothers. Not directly. Your wishes – yours and those of your deranged husband – are a terror we could never equal. Hence my silence, mum.

I didn't protect my brother, but I was assaulted too. I understood this only recently: our stepfather made me his victim too. My stepfather made me his prisoner. I'm also one of his victims. A victim of his corrupt perversity. I'm corrupted but not corrupt, mum.

Where were you all? What were you doing when we were foundering right before your eyes? You, the people I loved so much . . . what have you done since you found out?

★

Perhaps, as you yourself complained, mum, I was wrong to say nothing. Perhaps I should have spoken much sooner.

I've thought about that a lot. Your condemnation was the worst poison.

But deep inside, mum, I'm making progress and I know this: even if I had spoken, you wouldn't have left, Évelyne.

Some people will say you were from 'that generation'. But I think more crucially you were 'that sort of person'.

Do you really think I should have spoken up?

Look, mum: I'm doing it now.

I'm taking the risk, even if I can't breathe any more. I'm tearing myself away from Victor. At the risk of losing him. At the risk of hurting him even more.

My stepfather did too much harm to me too. By choosing my brother he created too many victims. Brothers and sisters muzzled by unreliable parents. An uncle, an aunt, cousins, children and grandchildren. Your grandchildren who had to cope, uncomprehending, with your sudden absence.

Look, mum. I'm writing for all the victims, the countless victims who are never mentioned because no one knows how to look them in the eye.

Mum, I've been suffocated by guilt, sadness and anger for all these years.

I was fourteen and I let it happen. I was fourteen and, by letting it happen, I might as well have done it myself. I was fourteen and I knew and I didn't say anything.

I was fourteen and I lied to you, mum. I was fourteen and I probably derived some pleasure from discovering a space I thought was forbidden.

I was fourteen, and if you're the sister, you shoulder the guilt to lighten your brother's load, you make it yours in order to release him. You imprison yourself.

I will always be the person best equipped to understand Victor's irrational guilt. I've lived with mine, every day, for thirty years.

Right up until the lively, humorous little girl that I was broke free of her mother and tried to poison the hydra by finishing this book.

– Paris, August 2020

For letting me write this book when all he wants is peace, my thanks to Victor.

This **brazen** book was created by

Publishing Director: Romilly Morgan
Translation: Adriana Hunter
Language Editor: Ellie Corbett
Senior Editor: Faye Robson
Assistant Editor: George Brooker
Creative Director: Jonathan Christie
Typesetter: Jouve (UK), Milton Keynes
Production Manager: Caroline Alberti
Sales: Kevin Hawkins, Marianne Laidlaw
Publicity: Megan Brown
Marketing: Rosa Patel
Legal: Simon Heilbron, Reviewed & Cleared